*In Search
of
Immortality*

Divine things are too deep to be expressed by common words. The heavenly teachings are expressed in parable in order to be understood and preserved for ages to come. When the spiritually minded dive deeply into the ocean of their meaning they bring to the surface the pearls of their inner significance. There is no greater pleasure than to study God's Word with a spiritual mind.

'Abdu'l-Bahá

In Search of Immortality

The journey and the goal ... the soul in this world

Geoffrey Gore

GEORGE RONALD
OXFORD

George Ronald, *Publisher*
Oxford
www.grbooks.com

©Geoffrey Gore 2010
All Rights Reserved

A catalogue record for this book is available from the British Library

ISBN 978–0–85398–545–7

CONTENTS

Why this book?		1
1	These brief moments	9
2	The limits of understanding	13
3	The soul in this world	31
4	Worlds of light	48
5	Spiritual quickening	63
6	The effect of veils	75
7	Soul, mind and spirit	85
8	Mind and the mental faculties	101
9	The struggle within	114
10	To seek and to find	126
11	The source of happiness	134
12	Departing this life	149
13	Life notes for the pilgrim	164
14	Bahá'u'lláh and the evolution of spiritual man	169
Epilogue: A tribute to my parents		187
Glossary of terms		189
Bibliography		191
Notes and references		195

WHY THIS BOOK?

It is part of the human condition to search for meaning. Man is the only creature that is self-aware, who knows that this earthly existence will inevitably end in death, and so, predictably, he asks the question 'Why are we here?'

To seek the meaning of life is also to seek the meaning of death, since death cannot be separated from life and if, like myself, you believe that the meaning of life goes far beyond what is immediately available to the senses, that there is a deeper, spiritual dimension to our existence, then you will also acknowledge that death is far more than the termination of the body.

This was also the view taken by Socrates, the great Greek philosopher who promoted the concept of the immortality of the human spirit and who asserted his belief that physical death would be a door leading to life in a completely different condition.

In the *Trial and Death of Socrates* there is a dialogue in which Cebes invites Socrates to convince him of the pre-existence and immortality of the soul. Socrates' response centres largely on the principle that everything has an opposite (honourable/base, just/unjust, greater/lesser, stronger/weaker, swifter/slower, etc.), that such opposites are generated one from the other, and therefore mortality presupposes immortality.

> Then if life and death are opposites, they are generated one from the other . . .[1]

He is further reported to have stated (in the *Phaedo*),

> Indeed, as I am setting out on a journey to the other world, what could be more fitting for me than to talk about my journey, and to consider what we imagine to be its nature? How could we better employ the interval between this and sunset?[2]

This sums up my own feeling about life and the reason for this book. What better subject could there be to discuss? Surely, talking about and writing about this life and preparing for the next world should be the most natural, comforting and constructive of things to do.

Socrates was, of course, an old man when he uttered these words, and had only a little time to live. He was, however, convinced that the way he lived his life was far more important than how long he lived. He asked his friend Crito,

> Now consider whether we still hold to the belief, that we should set the highest value, not on living, but on living well?

Crito agreed, 'Yes, we do.'[3] Then later in the dialogue, Socrates went on to say:

> And therefore I am not so much grieved at death: I am confident that the dead have some kind of existence, and, as has been said of old, an existence that is far better for the good than for the wicked.[4]

Socrates also discussed such compelling subjects as the way in which the body and its ' . . . passions, and desires, and fears . . .' hinder our pursuit of 'truth' and 'real being' and that 'pure knowledge' and 'wisdom' will come to us after death. 'For then, and not till then, will the soul exist by herself, separate from the body.'[5]

Socrates died still holding fast to the principles he espoused so vigorously. He was a seeker after truth who kept asking questions to the end of his life, challenging himself and all those around him in his attempt to understand everything he could about the condition of spiritual man. He is someone to whom most people can relate, because he wanted to find answers to those questions relating to the meaning of life.

In today's world the concept of 'spiritual man' has faded from most human institutions in the West. Organized religion as experienced by recent generations has increasingly been rejected; it is no longer perceived to be relevant. Of those who have remained in the church, many have joined offshoots of their faith, or moved into religious communities which they feel are more spiritually 'alive' and which share their personal views on spirituality.

Commenting on the condition of the world towards the end of the 19th century, Bahá'u'lláh wrote:

> The face of the world hath altered. The way of God and the religion of God have ceased to be of any worth in the eyes of men . . . The vitality of men's belief in God is dying out in every land . . . The corrosion of ungodliness is eating into the vitals of human society.[6]

From the early 20th century a materialistic interpretation of life became so entrenched in society that it proceeded with growing confidence to cut its ties with religion. 'God is dead' and 'religion is the opiate of the people' were phrases which reflected the widespread belief that somehow the constraints perceived to be associated with religion had been thrown off. Mankind had replaced God with science, a science which promised a tangible form of heaven on earth: better health, better food, better education, higher living standards – all contributing to human happiness and a secure, peaceful world.

So how is it that we now find ourselves in the 21st century living precariously in a world which appears in many respects to be disintegrating, where armed conflicts still abound, terrorist bombings are commonplace, corruption is widespread, public safety has declined, where millions die of malnutrition in poor countries, while in developed nations the consequences of human excesses, of over-eating and substance abuse place an enormous strain on health systems?

It is undeniable that science has benefited man, but those benefits have largely been reaped by the affluent few while huge numbers remain without even the basic necessities of life.

What is also evident is that behind the outward appearance of material progress, and cutting across all boundaries separating peoples, is a void. Many are experiencing an emptiness and lack of meaning which is reflected in addictions, neuroses, fears and anxieties.

Clearly something important is missing.

Science defines man as a biological–chemical entity, and makes no allowance for metaphysical matters. Human behaviour is seen in terms of the effects of 'nature and nurture', the influence of genes[7] on the one hand, and of environmental factors on the other. Such definitions take no account of the great spiritual forces influencing man or the all-important spiritual element of the human reality: the soul. It is knowledge of that spiritual reality that is missing in the lives of so many people.

Belief in God and belief in the concept of immortality are vanishing from the consciousness of those people living in materialistic, so-called 'developed' societies. What remains is a biological–chemical definition of man. A living man is seen as no different from a living animal, and death nothing more than the cessation of heartbeat, respiration and electrical activity in the brain. 'Life' is seen as physical life only; medical science attempts to prolong it, to save people from early death, and provides anti-depressants to enable people to cope with life; in short, to live with the emptiness.

Paradoxically, while that branch of society emphasizes the objective of prolonging life, violent death of every kind is the unvarying fare served up by the news media. We are exposed to brutal killing in every imaginable form through cinema, television, DVD and even in video games for children.

In spite of this undeniable interest in murder, pointless violence and the grossest aspects of human conduct, people do not have the same fascination with natural death. Death which comes naturally at the end of life is somehow made invisible, confined to the loneliness of a hospital ward or hospice bed, and its significance and real meaning is lost. Talking about death is considered to be morbid, while the knowledge that life is short is, to many, merely the justification for seeking wealth rather than wisdom, quantity rather than quality; it becomes an excuse for excess, a justification for attempts to stuff as much into life as possible without having any thought for the consequences of such actions. Many consciously avoid even thinking of their own deaths, a decision which increases the feeling of emptiness, and fills it with fear.

How we view death is important, if only for the fact that our attitude towards it will profoundly influence how we live. For instance, fear of death is debilitating and gives rise to all manner of neuroses which trouble people throughout their lives. The negative effects that such thinking has on the human psyche were identified by 'Abdu'l-Bahá almost 100 years ago:

> The conception of annihilation is a factor in human degradation, a cause of human debasement and lowliness, a source of human fear and abjection. It has been conducive to the dispersion and weakening of human thought whereas the realization of existence and continuity has upraised man to sublimity of ideals, established the foundations of human progress and stimulated the development of heavenly virtues; therefore it behooves man to abandon thoughts of non-existence and death which are absolutely imaginary and see himself ever-living,

everlasting in the divine purpose of his creation. He must turn away from ideas which degrade the human soul so that day by day and hour by hour he may advance upward and higher to spiritual perception of the continuity of the human reality. If he dwells upon the thought of non-existence he will become utterly incompetent; with weakened will-power his ambition for progress will be lessened and the acquisition of human virtues will cease.[8]

Belief in life after death and the immortality of the soul is common to all religions and also to the cultures of the many indigenous peoples throughout the world. Actually, life after death really means life after life, since death is only the bridge between this life and the next, just as childbirth is simply the event which connects life in the womb to life outside it.

The knowledge that comes through religion helps man to view physical death as a doorway to spiritual life and shows him that it should not be feared at all.

I have made death a messenger of joy to thee. Wherefore dost thou grieve?[9]

Life, death, the human soul, immortality . . . these are spiritual matters, and in the domain of the Prophets of God, those illumined figures who have left to us the legacy of their spoken and written word throughout history. Krishna, Buddha, Zoroaster, Abraham, Moses, Christ, Muhammad, and more recently, the Báb (1819–1850) and Bahá'u'lláh (1817–1892) – they are the spiritual teachers of mankind, the Ones most qualified to share knowledge and insight into the great questions of life. Anyone who believes in God will sooner or later come to appreciate that the knowledge revealed by the Prophets is a power which influences life in this world more than could ever be imagined.

The followers of all the major religions believe in the divine origin of the texts of their Faiths, referring to them as the Word of God. Close examination reveals that all the Messengers of God speak with the same voice, are inspired by the same divine force and appear for the sole purpose of advancing the process of the 'evolution of spiritual man' through educating the world of humanity. Hinduism, Buddhism, Judaism, Zoroastrianism, Christianity, Islam and the Bahá'í Faith – all of them are successive expressions of one religion, the religion of God.

The most recent spiritual episode in the life of humanity (the Revelation of Bahá'u'lláh) is associated with a great outpouring of knowledge, and this is significant for a number of reasons. Although belief in life after physical death is common to all religions, up until now very few references to the human soul could be found in the holy books. This has changed with the coming of Bahá'u'lláh. For the first time in religious history, subjects such as the soul, the mind, and the spiritual condition of man in this world have been explained in some depth, enabling man to better understand his true reality.

To know the meaning of life it is first necessary to know oneself, and my personal search to answer that question led me to the Bahá'í Faith and to investigate the life of Bahá'u'lláh. The truths contained in His Writings and the Writings of His son 'Abdu'l-Bahá influenced me profoundly – ultimately, it was transformative knowledge. Since then, it has been my conviction that the greatest gift one can give another person is to assist them to find the Word of God for themselves. For seekers of spiritual truth who have not previously come into contact with this power, discovering it can be a life-changing experience.

This book is my response to having received that gift; it explores the journey of life from a spiritual perspective and examines the forces that influence us as we prepare ourselves in this world for the next. It looks at soul, mind, spirit, the mental faculties, and a range of other subjects that seem to have a bearing on the meaning of life, and it includes many fascinating passages from the Words of God: some from the Old and New Testaments and the Qur'án, and a large number from the Bahá'í Writings – Words associated with the most recent episodes in the unfolding of the religion of God to man. Writings associated with earlier revelations, passed down over a long period of time in the form of oral traditions, such as the Buddhist and Hindu scriptures, have not been included here. All of these different Holy Scriptures refer to the immortality of man, yet it should be noted that while the Buddha referred to life after this life, interpretations placed on these sayings somehow gave rise to a widespread belief in the doctrine of reincarnation among many of His followers, a doctrine which is not upheld by any of the Messengers of God to Whose actual Writings we do have access.

The impossibility of reincarnation is explained in some detail in the Bahá'í Writings, and the following is an excerpt from one of those passages:

> The first argument for its impossibility is that the outward is the expression of the inward; the earth is the mirror of the Kingdom; the material world corresponds to the spiritual world. Now observe that in the sensible world appearances are not repeated, for no being in any respect is identical with, nor the same as, another being. The sign of singleness is visible and apparent in all things. If all the granaries of the world were full of grain, you would not find two grains absolutely alike, the same and identical without any distinction. It is certain that there will be differences and distinctions between them. As the proof of uniqueness exists in all things, and the Oneness and Unity of God is apparent in the reality of all things, the repetition of the same appearance is absolutely impossible. Therefore, reincarnation, which is the repeated appearance of the same spirit with its former essence and condition in this same world of appearance, is impossible and unrealizable. As the repetition of the same appearance is impossible and interdicted for each of the material beings, so for spiritual beings also, a return to the same condition, whether in the arc of descent or in the arc of ascent, is interdicted and impossible, for the material corresponds to the spiritual.
>
> . . . If we say that this reincarnation is for acquiring perfections so that matter may become refined and delicate, and that the light of the spirit may be manifest in it with the greatest perfection, this also is mere imagination. For, even supposing we believe in this argument, still change of nature is impossible through renewal and return. The essence of imperfection, by returning, does not become the reality of perfection; complete darkness, by returning, does not become the source of light; the essence of weakness is not transformed into power and might by returning, and an earthly nature does not become a heavenly reality.[10]

Man's attachments in this world, whether to objects or to ideas, have the same outcome – these things act as veils and cloud our awareness of God. The Word of God is a power that can remove those veils and free man to love God; it is an ocean of truth.

> The Word of God is the king of words and its pervasive influence is incalculable. It hath ever dominated and will continue to dominate the realm of being.[11]

Some people have the gift of assisting others to find the pearls contained in that ocean and in this connection I wish to pay special tribute to the inspiration, the understanding and the joy I have gained over many years from the books and recorded talks of the Bahá'í author Adib Taherzadeh (1921–2000). It is possible that I have used language or phrases which originate from insights gained from Mr Taherzadeh, and if I have done so without giving due acknowledgement to this source (or others), it is an unintentional discourtesy.

In the following pages I have quoted extensively from the Bahá'í Writings on a wide range of subjects, but for the sake of brevity I shall preface these quotations by simply using the words 'the Writings'. In all cases this denotes the Bahá'í Writings.

Whether you believe in God or a source of power beyond yourself, or an existence beyond just the physical or not, I hope that in the following pages you will find something that will challenge and inspire you as you continue your own life journey.

CHAPTER 1

THESE BRIEF MOMENTS

In this world, the soul dwells between darkness and light. The promptings of the higher nature make it seek after the world of the spirit while the influence of the lower nature, like gravity, pulls it downward, veils it from the light and makes it a captive of the material world. If those veils are removed, then a great spiritual journey begins – man becomes a seeker of immortality. The opportunity to begin that search and ultimately to satisfy the yearnings of the human spirit is available during this brief time spent as pilgrims on earth.

The pursuit of happiness

Happiness is a universal human goal and people will make sacrifices if necessary to achieve it, but opinions vary as to where real happiness is to be found. Those who view life as a business and their time as currency seek to find happiness in material success, but risk becoming unhappy and distressed if things do not go well for them. There are also those who choose to stop accumulating wealth and retire earlier from the demands of working life with a view to spending their remaining time in a more meaningful way. This 'lifestyle' decision not only reflects the desire to reduce stress and enjoy better health, it is for many a search for meaning and a search for happiness; it echoes that unspoken thought, 'there must be more to life than this'.

Those whose search leads them to religion find that the Messengers of God call attention to the spiritual significance of this earthly pilgrimage; they teach that the source of true happiness lies in neither health nor wealth, but in man's turning towards God in order to illuminate his higher nature. It is this mindfulness of God which helps combat the smothering effects of materialism which can so easily obscure the spiritual dimension.

Society has increasingly adopted the idea that the only measurable and therefore acceptable laws governing life are the physical laws. In contrast to this, religious truth focuses on the equally potent spiritual laws influencing life in this world, and challenges man to follow the pathway to God. Logically, since man is influenced by both physical and spiritual forces that all originate from the same source, the knowledge of both should be taught. On that basis, discussing God and spiritual subjects should be commonplace, a natural part of daily life, yet in practice, society has increasingly excluded spirituality from the mainstream of life. So much so, that even within families, one who professes a belief in God is often treated with disdain by those who do not. Years may pass with no acknowledgement of this difference in outlook between the members of a family, who in most other respects have reason to be very close.

To deny the spiritual character of man is to deny his immortality and the possibility of achieving real happiness. All things connected with the material world are by their very nature temporary, and therefore the pleasures coming from them will be temporary. In contrast, the spiritual world bestows benefits that are lasting and satisfying. In the human soul, which originates from the spiritual worlds, that faculty concerned with the acquiring of spiritual qualities can only be awakened by the breath of God, the power referred to by the Prophets as the Holy Spirit. Once awakened, the development of this spiritual side of man's nature satisfies the soul's yearning, gives meaning to life and opens the door to happiness in this world.

Were it not for the examples of the great spiritual teachers of humanity, it would be easy to point to the imperfections of this world and become cynical and negative, but their lives of sacrifice have illumined the pathway to spiritual growth and revealed that, in spite of its condition, this world is an ideal testing ground for souls. It is a place where human beings can acquire perfections. If this physical existence is the precursor to a spiritual existence, if this life is only the 'first life' and a place to prepare for the continuing journey of the soul, and if this life turns out to be the one where choices really matter, then the most important issue for the individual in this life becomes how to best prepare for the next life.

A time of preparation

God sends His Messengers to this world to help man; They illumine the pathway of life and help us to acquire spiritual attributes. The soul takes these attributes into the next world because they are necessary for its continuing progress, much as the foetus develops organs in the womb in preparation for life in this world. Consequently, if the soul fails to acquire attributes before its entry into the spiritual worlds, its progress will be affected; it will be held back by a lack of power.

In this world power is associated with money, influence and the control of resources. A person's value and consequently status in society are generally determined by his material assets. Greater importance is placed on the opinion of those with the highest academic qualifications; greater value is attached to those with outstanding physical qualities, such as beauty, sports skills or strength. In contrast to this, the Messengers of God put emphasis on spiritual power, on the development of spiritual attributes and divine qualities.

> Training in morals and good conduct is far more important than book learning. A child that is cleanly, agreeable, of good character, well-behaved – even though he be ignorant – is preferable to a child that is rude, unwashed, ill-natured, and yet becoming deeply versed in all the sciences and arts. The reason for this is that the child who conducts himself well, even though he be ignorant, is of benefit to others, while an ill-natured, ill-behaved child is corrupted and harmful to others, even though he be learned. If, however, the child be trained to be both learned and good, the result is light upon light.[1]

Good character may not bring fame or fortune, and society may not view spiritual qualities as having exceptional value, but they are the source of man's happiness in this world and are the essential acquisitions needed by man for life in the next world.

Sadly, it is often not until someone's physical life comes to an end that the importance of spiritual qualities becomes most apparent. Regardless of country or culture, the things which mourners are drawn to remember are the attributes which that person possessed, the degree to which he or she manifested such qualities as kindness, courage, generosity and so on. However, rather than continuing to pray for the progress of that soul in the next world after its passing, the current fashion is to regard a funeral as the final remembrance. Friends and family gather to 'celebrate the life of . . .', as if a collection of memories of the few years spent on earth between the moments of birth and death is all that remains, the sum total of a human being. But there is much more to man; 'man is, in reality, a spiritual being,'[2] deserving to be treated as ever-living, since the soul continues on, remaining unaffected by the death of the physical body. It is this spiritual dimension of man that will be explored in the following chapters.

Dealing with death

> Ye are even as the unwary bird that with full confidence warbleth upon the bough; till of a sudden the fowler Death throws it upon the dust, and the melody, the form and the colour are gone, leaving not a trace.[3]

To be young is to feel invincible. With the anticipation of a lifetime ahead and so much to learn, experience and accomplish, most young people are totally focused on the moment, here and now. No need to contemplate how precarious this existence is, because the natural focus in childhood and youth is on life; therefore, the mind disregards ideas of mortality. Even as the years pass, it is difficult to imagine that one day this human body will not be here; instead, people automatically hold to the belief that there is still plenty of time.

That is, until death arrives unannounced, a reminder to those left behind that there may not be as much time as was thought.

> For what is your life? It is even a vapour, that appeareth for a little time, and then vanisheth away.[4]

The importance of the brief time spent in this world is that man may discover his true self and reveal the spiritual power that lies hidden within the soul. Discovering the true self gives man purpose; it motivates him to live life in a way that brings happiness. When man understands that he is immortal and that life here is a preparation for death, he will no longer find fear in the fact that his death is inevitable.

CHAPTER 2

THE LIMITS OF UNDERSTANDING

> His [God's] is another realm, and of that realm no understanding can be won. No access can be gained thereto; all entry is forbidden there. The utmost one can say is that Its existence can be proved, but the conditions of Its existence are unknown.[1]

This chapter will look briefly at the limits of human understanding, and the role played by the Prophets in bridging the void between man and God – that void which reflects man's inability to comprehend God.

Yes, there are definite limits, yet the knowledge that man has been given the capacity to prove the existence of God and of the 'realm of God' through the mind's powers of discovery should be a source of great encouragement. A wealth of knowledge has been made available in the Writings of Bahá'u'lláh and 'Abdu'l-Bahá. These Writings offer the opportunity to learn of God and to prove the existence of God by the power of reasoning; a lifetime of study would not be sufficient to absorb it all.

> Thus man cannot grasp the Essence of Divinity, but can, by his reasoning power, by observation, by his intuitive faculties and the revealing power of his faith, believe in God, discover the bounties of His Grace. He becometh certain that though the Divine Essence is unseen of the eye, and the existence of the Deity is intangible, yet conclusive spiritual proofs assert the existence of that unseen Reality.[2]

This great outpouring of knowledge was spoken of by Daniel in the Old Testament:

> And he said, Go thy way, Daniel: for the words are closed up and sealed till the time of the end.[3]

and by Christ as recorded in the New Testament:

> I have yet many things to say unto you, but ye cannot bear them now. Howbeit when he, the Spirit of truth, is come, he will guide you into all truth: for he shall not speak of himself; but whatsoever he shall hear, that shall he speak: and he will shew you things to come.[4]

The Writings contain many proofs regarding the existence of God and of the spiritual worlds of God, and it is to these proofs that man must apply the God-given faculty of mind and the power of understanding which arises from the soul. Faith is no longer 'blind faith'. Reason and logic can open the door to a deeper understanding of the nature of the relationship between the human soul and its Creator.

> These are rational proofs; in this age the peoples of the world need the arguments of reason.[5]

Example of a rational proof

One example of the proof of the existence of God can be found in 'Abdu'l-Bahá's explanation regarding composition and decomposition. He examines three possibilities: namely, that the composition of things in the world could be accidental, involuntary or voluntary, and then by reasoning shows how all existing phenomena are the product of an unseen universal intelligence. The following is an excerpt from His talk.

> The power of attraction has as its function attractive, or magnetic, qualities. We cannot separate attraction from that power. The power of repulsion has as its function repelling – sending off. You cannot separate the effect from the cause. If these premises be true – and they are self-evident – then it would be impossible for a composite being, for the elements which have gone into the makeup of a composite organism, ever to be decomposed because the inherent nature of each element would be to hold fast together. As fire cannot be separated from heat, likewise the elemental being could not be subjected to decomposition, and this does not hold true because we see decomposition everywhere. Hence this theory is untrue, inasmuch as we observe that after each composition there is a process of decomposition which forever ends

it. By this we learn that composition as regards phenomena is neither accidental nor involuntary.

Then what have we left as a form of composition? It is the voluntary form of composition, which means that composition is effected through a superior will, that there is will expressed in this motive or action.[6]

The existence of a universal power

> ... whereas ye can see that this endless creation carrieth out its functions in perfect order, every separate part of it performing its own task with complete reliability, nor is there any flaw to be found in all its workings. Thus it is clear that a Universal Power existeth, directing and regulating this infinite universe. Every rational mind can grasp this fact.[7]

This 'Universal Power' operating throughout the entire creation is referred to in the Writings as the love of God: 'Love is the conscious bestowal of God, the bond of affiliation in all phenomena.'[8]

If the operation of the law of love ceased for a moment, then creation itself would likewise cease since the whole of creation exists only through the bounty of God. In the following Tablet, love is referred to as a light, a power, a law and a magnetic force:

> Know thou of a certainty that Love is the secret of God's holy Dispensation, the manifestation of the All-Merciful, the fountain of spiritual outpourings. Love is heaven's kindly light, the Holy Spirit's eternal breath that vivifieth the human soul. Love is the cause of God's revelation unto man, the vital bond inherent, in accordance with the divine creation, in the realities of things. Love is the one means that ensureth true felicity both in this world and the next. Love is the light that guideth in darkness, the living link that uniteth God with man, that assureth the progress of every illumined soul. Love is the most great law that ruleth this mighty and heavenly cycle, the unique power that bindeth together the divers elements of this material world, the supreme magnetic force that directeth the movements of the spheres in the celestial realms. Love revealeth with unfailing and limitless power the mysteries latent in the universe. Love is the spirit of life unto the adorned body of mankind, the establisher of true civilization in this

mortal world, and the shedder of imperishable glory upon every high-aiming race and nation.[9]

Love manifests in different degrees

'Abdu'l-Bahá specifically describes the law of love as the 'power of attraction' manifested throughout the kingdoms of creation, and further observed:

> We declare that love is the cause of the existence of all phenomena and that the absence of love is the cause of disintegration or non-existence.[10]

In another instance, He referred to this law and this power simply as 'spirit':

> The greatest power in the realm and range of human existence is spirit – the divine breath which animates and pervades all things. It is manifested throughout creation in different degrees or kingdoms.[11]

Simply put, without this animating power nothing would have life; seeds could not grow, creatures could not exist. It is the operation of this spirit or spiritual power which underlies the functioning or expression of all phenomena in creation.

The following excerpts[12] define how these different degrees of the power of love are expressed in the world:

Mineral kingdom

> This stone is the lowest degree of phenomena, but nevertheless within it a power of attraction is manifest without which the stone could not exist. This power of attraction in the mineral world is love, the only expression of love the stone can manifest.

Vegetable kingdom

> ... furthermore, the plant has the power of absorption from the earth. This is a higher degree of attraction which differentiates the plant from the mineral. In the kingdom of the vegetable this is an expression of love, the highest capacity of expression the vegetable possesses. By this power of attraction, or augmentation, the plant grows day by day.

Animal kingdom

Then we come to the animal world, which is still higher in degree than the vegetable kingdom. In it the power of love makes itself still more manifest. The light of love is more resplendent in the animal kingdom because the power of attraction whereby elements cohere and cellular atoms commingle now reveals itself in certain emotions and sensibilities which produce instinctive fellowship and association.

Human kingdom

Finally, we reach the kingdom of man. Here we find that all the degrees of the mineral, vegetable and animal expressions of love are present plus unmistakable attractions of consciousness. That is to say, man is the possessor of a degree of attraction which is conscious and spiritual. Here is an immeasurable advance. In the human kingdom spiritual susceptibilities come into view, love exercises its superlative degree, and this is the cause of human life.

This expression of love in different degrees throughout creation provides us with further proof of the existence of God and also explains why there are limits to our understanding.

The principle of 'limitations of degree'

Although the Words of God contain an ocean of wisdom, it must be acknowledged that there are some things which cannot be known because they are beyond us; they are above us in the hierarchy of creation.

The kingdoms of God are either phenomenal or they are essential. The phenomenal or physical kingdoms are by definition temporary and subject to decay and change, to death and decomposition, while the essential kingdoms of God are not subject to decline and are completely beyond our comprehension.

In the physical world, every created thing functions within the limits placed on its existence. At the lower level is the mineral kingdom, followed by the vegetable kingdom. Above this is the animal kingdom which is superseded by the human kingdom. These are the kingdoms of the phenomenal or material world, and each one is definitely limited as to its capacity. While having a capacity superior to those beneath, the principle of limitations of degree prevents each kingdom from being able to encompass or comprehend the kingdom(s) above it. This difference in capacity '... is a hindrance to comprehension'.[13]

> Minerals, plants and animals are bereft of the mental faculties of man that discover the realities of all things, but man himself comprehendeth all the stages beneath him. Every superior stage comprehendeth that which is inferior and discovereth the reality thereof, but the inferior one is unaware of that which is superior and cannot comprehend it.[14]

> It is evident, therefore, that difference in degree is ever an obstacle to comprehension of the higher by the lower, the superior by the inferior.[15]

This principle of limitations of degree demonstrates that having no knowledge of something is no proof of its non-existence. 'Abdu'l-Bahá explains this further:

> To however great a degree the plant may have evolved, it is unable to understand the animal world; this ignorance is no proof that the animal does not exist!
> The animal, be he ever so highly developed, cannot imagine the intelligence of man, neither can he realize the nature of his soul. But, again, this does not prove that man is without intellect, or without soul. It only demonstrates this, that one form of existence is incapable of comprehending a form superior to itself.
> This flower may be unconscious of such a being as man, but the fact of its ignorance does not prevent the existence of humanity.[16]

The same logic must be applied to the separation between the 'human world' and the 'world of spirit', that is, *just because it cannot be seen does not mean that it is not there!*

> In the same way, if materialists do not believe in the existence of the soul, their unbelief does not prove that there is no such realm as the world of spirit. The very existence of man's intelligence proves his immortality; moreover, darkness proves the presence of light, for without light there would be no shadow. Poverty proves the existence

of riches, for, without riches, how could we measure poverty? Ignorance proves that knowledge exists, for without knowledge how could there be ignorance?

Therefore the idea of mortality presupposes the existence of immortality – for if there were no Life Eternal, there would be no way of measuring the life of this world![17]

The spiritual worlds of God are out of our reach

The human kingdom, although far superior to the animal kingdom, is restricted. Beyond the physical world are other degrees of existence which we cannot comprehend. They are referred to in the Writings as the spiritual worlds of God and are set apart from this world; they are eternal, unlimited, divine, and cannot be seen or experienced by the outward senses. The only way that anything at all can be learned about those worlds is through the knowledge revealed by the Messengers of God and through our understanding of the divine attributes which They manifest, and even that understanding is strictly limited by our human capacity.

'Abdu'l-Bahá states:

> This knowledge of the attributes is also proportioned to the capacity and power of man; it is not absolute.[18]

It must be conceded then, that the true essence of God is 'unseen, inaccessible, and unknowable'.[19]

Even the essential reality of the physical world is beyond us

Having accepted that our ability to grasp the reality of the spiritual world is inadequate, it must also be acknowledged that even the reality of the physical world around us is difficult to penetrate. 'Abdu'l-Bahá said:

> . . . our knowledge of things, even of created and limited things, is knowledge of their qualities and not of their essence . . .[20]

When we consider the world of existence, we find that the essential reality underlying any given phenomenon is unknown. Phenomenal, or created, things are known to us only by their attributes. Man discerns only manifestations, or attributes, of objects, while the identity, or reality, of them remains hidden.[21]

Bahá'u'lláh explains that the realities of all created things are concealed by veils and that when those veils are removed, nothing will remain except 'the Sign of God':

> It is clear and evident that when the veils that conceal the realities of the manifestations of the Names and Attributes of God, nay of all created things visible or invisible, have been rent asunder, nothing except the Sign of God will remain – a sign which He, Himself, hath placed within these realities.[22]

Balanced against these imposed limits is the knowledge that there is a connection between this life and the next and it is evident that it was always God's purpose that man should acknowledge His existence, since in one of the prayers revealed by Bahá'u'lláh we read:

> Thou didst wish to make Thyself known unto men; therefore, Thou didst, through a word of Thy mouth, bring creation into being and fashion the universe.[23]

And in the short obligatory prayer also revealed by Bahá'u'lláh are the words:

> I bear witness, O my God, that Thou hast created me to know Thee and to worship Thee.[24]

Human minds may not be able to comprehend His creation, yet plainly the entire universe provides overwhelming evidence of the love of God towards His creation.

> How bewildering to me, insignificant as I am, is the attempt to fathom the sacred depths of Thy knowledge! How futile my efforts to visualize the magnitude of the power inherent in Thine handiwork – the revelation of Thy creative power! How can mine eye, which hath no faculty to perceive itself, claim to have discerned Thine Essence, and how can mine heart, already powerless to apprehend the significance of its own potentialities, pretend to have comprehended Thy nature? How can I

claim to have known Thee, when the entire creation is bewildered by Thy mystery, and how can I confess not to have known Thee, when, lo, the whole universe proclaimeth Thy Presence and testifieth to Thy truth?[25]

If we wish to come in touch with the reality of Divinity, we do so by recognizing its phenomena, its attributes and traces, which are widespread in the universe. All things in the world of phenomena are expressive of that one reality. Its lights are shining, its heat is manifest, its power is expressive, and its education, or training, resplendent everywhere.[26]

Man is not bound by the laws of nature

All things in the phenomenal world are bound by the laws of nature except man.

> The animal is the captive of nature and cannot transgress the rules and laws thereof. In man, however, there is a discovering power that transcendeth the world of nature and controlleth and interfereth with the laws thereof. For instance, all minerals, plants and animals are captives of nature. The sun itself with all its majesty is so subservient to nature that it hath no will of its own and cannot deviate a hair's-breadth from the laws thereof. In like manner all other beings, whether of the mineral, the vegetable or the animal world, cannot deviate from the laws of nature, nay, all are the slaves thereof. Man, however, though in body the captive of nature is yet free in his mind and soul, and hath the mastery over nature.[27]

Man, unlike the animal, is endowed with that extraordinary power, the power of the mind. He interferes with the natural laws and seeks to understand and explain the physical world.

Creation: Testing the limits of our understanding

Today, it is widely accepted that the universe started from a 'singularity'— that point in time when all matter and all physical laws were one, prior to what is usually described by physicists as the 'big bang'. It is interesting to note, in this connection, an excerpt from a Tablet written by Bahá'u'lláh referring to the common origin of what He calls the 'active force' and its 'recipient'. He declares that both were created by the 'Word of God', the Cause of all existence.

> The world of existence came into being through the heat generated from the interaction between the active force and that which is its recipient. These two are the same, yet they are different . . . Such as communicate the generating influence and such as receive its impact are indeed created through the irresistible Word of God which is the Cause of the entire creation, while all else besides His Word are but the creatures and the effects thereof.
>
> Know thou, moreover, that the Word of God – exalted be His glory – is higher and far superior to that which the senses can perceive, for it is sanctified from any property or substance. It transcendeth the limitations of known elements and is exalted above all the essential and recognized substances. It became manifest without any syllable or sound and is none but the Command of God which pervadeth all created things. It hath never been withheld from the world of being. It is God's all-pervasive grace, from which all grace doth emanate. It is an entity far removed above all that hath been and shall be.[28]

In 'Abdu'l-Bahá's talk regarding the beginning of matter and the appearance of beings, there is a similar statement.

> . . . it is evident that in the beginning matter was one, and that one matter appeared in different aspects in each element. Thus various forms were produced, and these various aspects as they were produced became permanent, and each element was specialized. But this permanence was not definite, and did not attain realization and perfect existence until after a very long time. Then these elements became composed, and organized and combined in infinite forms; or rather from the composition and combination of these elements innumerable beings appeared.[29]

The endless universe

Scientists have calculated that the momentous 'birth' of our universe occurred approximately 15 billion years ago; therefore Bahá'u'lláh's statement quoted above: '*The world of existence came into being . . .*'³⁰ could be taken to be a description of what happened after the 'big bang', yet in another passage from His writings Bahá'u'lláh says:

> As to thy question concerning the origin of creation. Know assuredly that God's creation hath existed from eternity, and will continue to exist forever. Its beginning hath had no beginning, and its end knoweth no end.³¹

He confirms that elements have become composed and matter has assumed different forms, but nowhere does He state that there was a time when nothing existed at all. Can any mind understand how something can have no beginning or end? No.³²

Man is 'created', consequently no matter how hard he might try, he will never be able to grasp the 'Creator'. Those who are having difficulty reconciling these passages may take heart from this further statement on the subject from the pen of 'Abdu'l-Bahá:

> Know that it is one of the most abstruse spiritual truths that the world of existence – that is to say, this endless universe – has no beginning.³³

Can your mind imagine 15 billion years ago or before a 'singularity'? No.

Regarding this principle of the endless universe 'Abdu'l-Bahá further explains that:

> The power of God is eternal and there have always been beings to manifest it; that is why we say that the worlds of God are infinite – there has never been a time when they did not exist.³⁴

> The names the Powerful, the Living, the Provider, the Creator require and necessitate the existence of creatures. If there were no creatures, Creator would be meaningless. If there were none to provide for, we could not think of the Provider. If there were no life, the Living would be beyond the power of conception. Therefore, all the names and attributes of God require the existence of objects or creatures upon which they have been bestowed and in which they have become manifest. If there was a time when no creation existed, when there was none to provide for, it would imply a time when there was no existent One,

no Trainer, and the attributes and qualities of God would have been meaningless and without significance.[35]

Our finite minds

Our own solar system forms a small part of a star system so big that it is difficult for anyone to comprehend the size of it, let alone to conceive what lies beyond it. The universe is said to be made up of hundreds of millions of these galaxies, each containing many billions of stars. Can your mind imagine what lies beyond the furthermost constellations, outside the expanding universe? No, these are all concepts which cannot be grasped because human minds are 'finite' and 'strictly subjected' to 'limitations'.[36]

> Consider the endless phenomena of His creation. They are infinite; the universe is infinite. Who shall declare its height, its depth and length? It is absolutely infinite.[37]

> Every single manifestation of the myriad forms of creation is a reflection of the divine emanations, therefore the divine emanations are infinite, unlimited and illimitable. Gaze upward through immeasurable space to the majestic order of the colossal suns. These luminous bodies are numberless. Behind our solar system there are unfathomable stellar systems and above those stellar systems are the remote aggregations of the milky way. Extend your vision beyond the fixed stars and again you shall behold many spheres of light. In brief, the creation of the Almighty is beyond the grasp of the human intellect . . . When the reflection or physical creation is infinite, how is it possible to circumscribe the reality which is the basis of divine creation? The spiritual world is so much greater than the physical that in comparison with it the physical world is non-existent.[38]

No direct tie to the Creator

Knowing that the kingdom of God is essential (eternal, unknowable, divine) and that the kingdom of creation, by contrast, is phenomenal (physical and subject to decay and disintegration), it follows that no direct relationship can be possible between these kingdoms; as 'Abdu'l-Bahá says, 'It is self-evidently an impossibility.'[39]

THE LIMITS OF UNDERSTANDING

> No tie of direct intercourse can possibly bind Him to His creatures. He standeth exalted beyond and above all separation and union, all proximity and remoteness. No sign can indicate His presence or His absence; inasmuch as by a word of His command all that are in heaven and on earth have come to exist, and by His wish, which is the Primal Will itself, all have stepped out of utter nothingness into the realm of being, the world of the visible.[40]

Something which has been created can never hope to understand the force which brought it into being, just as the sculpture cannot know the sculptor, or the watch know the watchmaker.

> All that is in heaven and all that is in the earth have come to exist at His bidding, and by His Will all have stepped out of utter nothingness into the realm of being. How can, therefore, the creature which the Word of God hath fashioned comprehend the nature of Him Who is the Ancient of Days?[41]

As man cannot know what the essential attributes of 'God' are, it must be concluded that whatever understanding he *does* come to will be utterly inadequate, since this will be 'a pure product of imagination . . .'[42]

Of course, this fact does not stop the desire to know more. Questions arise because the soul yearns to know its creator, but however much effort is made, all are bound by the principle that 'the limited can never comprehend, surround, nor take in the unlimited'.[43] This explains why many questions cannot be answered, and it represents one of the logical proofs of the existence of God!

The intermediaries, who bestow understanding on man

Since no direct connection to God is possible, He (God) provided intermediaries to enable man to acquire knowledge of Him. Referred to as 'heavenly Messengers' and 'Shepherds of humanity', these pure Souls have become known to humanity as the great Messengers of God: Abraham, Moses, Buddha, Zoroaster, Krishna, Christ, Muhammad, the Báb and Bahá'u'lláh; They are the Revealers of the light of God to man from age to age.

Bahá'u'lláh explains that if it were not for the appearance of these divine

Messengers in the world, man would not be able to recognize the signs and attributes of God.

> And since there can be no tie of direct intercourse to bind the one true God with His creation, and no resemblance whatever can exist between the transient and the Eternal, the contingent and the Absolute, He hath ordained that in every age and dispensation a pure and stainless Soul be made manifest in the kingdoms of earth and heaven. Unto this subtle, this mysterious and ethereal Being He hath assigned a twofold nature; the physical, pertaining to the world of matter, and the spiritual, which is born of the substance of God Himself.[44]

> And when Thou didst purpose to make Thyself known unto men, Thou didst successively reveal the Manifestations of Thy Cause, and ordained each to be a sign of Thy Revelation among Thy people, and the Day-Spring of Thine invisible Self amidst Thy creatures . . .[45]

These intermediaries have literally been '*Mouthpieces of God*',[46] the Revealers of His Word. Christ made this abundantly clear in the statement:

> . . . he that hath seen me hath seen the Father . . . the words that I speak unto you I speak not of myself: but the Father that dwelleth in me, he doeth the works.[47]

While Bahá'u'lláh declared:

> This thing is not from Me, but from One Who is Almighty and All-Knowing. And He bade Me lift up My voice between earth and heaven, and for this there befell Me what hath caused the tears of every man of understanding to flow.[48]

> And whenever I chose to hold my peace and be still, lo, the voice of the Holy Ghost, standing on my right hand, aroused me, and the Supreme Spirit appeared before my face, and Gabriel overshadowed me, and the Spirit of Glory stirred within my bosom, bidding me arise and break my silence.[49]

God's love for man

God's love for man is the cause of creation; the existence of all phenomena is absolutely connected with the appearance of man, because man is potentially the highest expression of the love of God in the universe.

'If man did not exist,' 'Abdu'l-Bahá states, 'the universe would be without result, for the object of existence is the appearance of the perfections of God.'[50]

How humbling and how inspiring to think that God has provided an endless universe of great beauty and complexity within which the human reality can grow and develop the potential He has placed within it.

God has endowed man with a remarkable spiritual capacity, but the mystical attraction of the human soul to its Creator could not have been realized without the Messengers who have acted as His agents. This is why They are referred to as 'the greatest bounties of God in this phenomenal world'.[51]

> It is the warmth that these Luminaries of God generate, and the undying fires they kindle, which cause the light of the love of God to burn fiercely in the heart of humanity.[52]

> Were it not for the love of God, the hearts would not be illumined. Were it not for the love of God, the pathway of the Kingdom would not be opened. Were it not for the love of God, the Holy Books would not have been revealed. Were it not for the love of God, the divine Prophets would not have been sent to the world. The foundation of all these bestowals is the love of God. Therefore, in the human world there is no greater power than the love of God.[53]

This love of God for man is evident in many of the Writings revealed by Bahá'u'lláh, especially in His book *Hidden Words*:

> O Son of Man! Veiled in My immemorial being and in the ancient eternity of My essence, I knew My love for thee; therefore I created thee, have engraved upon thee Mine image and revealed to thee My beauty.[54]

> Thou art My lamp and My light is in thee . . .[55]

A covenant of love

> The purpose of God in creating man hath been, and will ever be, to enable him to know his Creator and to attain His Presence.[56]

The relationship between the Creator and humanity has been described as a covenant – an agreement between two parties. 'Love Me, that I may love thee,' Bahá'u'lláh reveals.[57]

The Messengers of God radiate God's love upon mankind; by accepting that love and by acknowledging its source, man will enter into that covenant, come to love that light and subsequently to develop spiritual capacity.

> O Son of Man! I loved thy creation, hence I created thee. Wherefore, do thou love Me, that I may name thy name and fill thy soul with the spirit of life.[58]

> I have breathed within thee a breath of My own Spirit, that thou mayest be My lover . . .[59]

God has promised that this flow of love will never stop, that the appearance of His Manifestations or Messengers in the human world throughout history is a never-ending process.

> Just as the surface of the material world becomes dark and dreary, the soil dormant, the trees naked and bare and no beauty or freshness remains to cheer the darkness and desolation, so the winter of the spiritual cycle witnesses the death and disappearance of divine growth and extinction of the light and love of God. But again the cycle begins and a new springtime appears. In it the former springtime has returned; the world is resuscitated, illumined and attains spirituality; religion is renewed and reorganized, hearts are turned to God, the summons of God is heard, and life is again bestowed upon man.[60]

Becoming attached to names

In holding fast to their 'own' Messenger, the followers of many religions today deny and exclude all the other Messengers of God who have appeared either before or afterwards, each one somehow taking the view that their own Messenger is unique and final. These people seem unwilling to accept the possibility that divine revelation is continuous; whereas it is evident that the Messengers of God appear from the same horizon and receive their inspiration from the same source. Clearly, God is not in competition with Himself. The pronouncements on this subject are among some of the most strongly worded passages contained in the Writings.

> Thou art surely aware of their idle contention, that all Revelation is ended, that the portals of Divine mercy are closed, that from the day-springs of eternal holiness no sun shall rise again, that the Ocean of everlasting bounty is forever stilled, and that out of the Tabernacle of ancient glory the Messengers of God have ceased to be made manifest. Such is the measure of the understanding of these small-minded, contemptible people. These people have imagined that the flow of God's all-encompassing grace and plenteous mercies, the cessation of which no mind can contemplate, has been halted.[61]

> By holding fast unto names they deprive themselves of the inner reality and by clinging to vain imaginings they are kept back from the Day-spring of heavenly signs.[62]

Human beings have always tried to limit God, whereas God is infinite:

> Prescribing limitation to God is human ignorance. God is the Ancient, the Almighty; His attributes are infinite. He is God because His light, His sovereignty, is infinite. If He can be limited to human ideas, He is not God. Strange it is that, notwithstanding these are self-evident truths, man continues to build walls and fences of limitation about God, about Divinity so glorious, illimitable, boundless . . . How could an almighty sovereignty, a Divinity so wondrous, be brought within the limitations of faulty human minds even as to terms and definition? Shall we then say that God has performed a certain thing and He will never be able to perform it again? That the Sun of His effulgence once shone upon the world but now has set forever? That His mercy, His grace, His bounty once descended but now have ceased? Is this possible? No! We can never say nor believe with truth that His Manifestation, the adored verity, the Sun of Reality, shall cease to shine upon the world.[63]

Knowledge of God through His attributes

> How shall we know God? We know Him by His attributes. We know Him by His signs. We know Him by His names.[64]

Even man's understanding of the signs, the names and the attributes of God is, however, strictly relative to the human capacity. What man sees is the limited expression of an unlimited power beyond his comprehension.

> Knowing God, therefore, means the comprehension and the knowledge of His attributes, and not of His Reality. This knowledge of the attributes is also proportioned to the capacity and power of man; it is not absolute.[65]

> O Son of Beauty! By My spirit and by My favour! By My mercy and by My beauty! All that I have revealed unto thee with the tongue of power, and have written for thee with the pen of might, hath been in accordance with thy capacity and understanding, not with My state and the melody of My voice.[66]

To summarize, while there are obvious limits to man's understanding, God has invested man with the capacity to know and to love God. The only way that man can know of God is by His attributes, and so God has ordained that in every age a pure soul appears to reflect those divine attributes, not only in His words but also in His life, providing a perfect example to mankind.

CHAPTER 3

THE SOUL IN THIS WORLD

The soul and the analogy of the child in the womb

The Prophets of God, who are the teachers of humanity, often used analogies to explain spiritual concepts, pointing to counterparts in the material world. For example, the principle of preparing our spiritual selves for a new existence beyond this physical world has a counterpart in the development of the child in its mother's womb.

The womb is not the home of the body, because the body is destined to be born into this world of existence. Likewise, this world is not the home of the soul. The soul, being a spiritual entity and 'essential' (emanating from God), is destined to cross over from the human kingdom into the spiritual kingdom at the moment of death.

The child will grow and develop through nine months in preparation for leaving the womb and cannot comprehend the existence of the world outside the womb. Similarly, the human reality cannot comprehend the next world, yet the brief time spent in this physical world is our opportunity to develop spiritually in preparation for the life which comes after death. Just as the event of birth brings our bodies into this physical world, the moment of physical death launches our spiritual selves into a spiritual world.

There is, however, a fundamental difference in the preparation period leading up to these two birthing events. In the world of the womb, development of the essential physical attributes in preparation for life in this world happens automatically; whereas acquiring the essential *spiritual* attributes in preparation for life in the next world requires effort on our part.

The development of the soul in preparation for the next world is subject to free will, to the choices made throughout our lives, choices that take on far greater meaning once it is recognized that we are 'standing in the balance'. To fulfil our potential, effort and perseverance are required; it is up to us, our volition.

> Know thou that all men have been created in the nature made by God, the Guardian, the Self-Subsisting. Unto each one hath been prescribed a pre-ordained measure, as decreed in God's mighty and guarded Tablets. All that which ye potentially possess can, however, be manifested only as a result of your own volition.[1]

Although the exact time of our leaving this world is not known to us, what is known is that leaving it is inevitable, and so it makes sense to do whatever we can to prepare adequately for the journey.

Between darkness and light

Although the human kingdom shares with the animal kingdom the outward senses of the body, humans also possess the distinguishing faculty of the rational soul which is an emanation from the worlds of God. Being both phenomenal (having a physical body) and essential (having a spiritual reality), we have a lower nature and a higher nature. This fact creates a tension within human beings, since the physical or animal side of our nature is drawn strongly to the material world, whilst the spiritual aspect arising from the soul is drawn towards the spiritual worlds of God.

> For the inner reality of man is a demarcation line between the shadow and the light . . .[2]

In effect, man is standing in the balance.

> As we have before indicated, this human reality stands between the higher and the lower in man, between the world of the animal and the world of Divinity. When the animal proclivity in man becomes predominant, he sinks even lower than the brute. When the heavenly powers are triumphant in his nature, he becomes the noblest and most superior being in the world of creation. All the imperfections found in the animal are found in man. In him there is antagonism, hatred and selfish struggle for existence; in his nature lurk jealousy, revenge, ferocity, cunning, hypocrisy, greed, injustice and tyranny. So to speak, the reality of man is clad in the outer garment of the animal, the habiliments of the world of nature, the world of darkness, imperfections and unlimited baseness.

> On the other hand, we find in him justice, sincerity, faithfulness, knowledge, wisdom, illumination, mercy and pity, coupled with intellect, comprehension, the power to grasp the realities of things and the ability to penetrate the truths of existence. All these great perfections are to be found in man. Therefore, we say that man is a reality which stands between light and darkness. From this standpoint his nature is threefold: animal, human and divine. The animal nature is darkness; the heavenly is light in light.[3]

The reality of man exists between opposing principles:

> Man is in the highest degree of materiality, and at the beginning of spirituality – that is to say, he is the end of imperfection and the beginning of perfection. He is at the last degree of darkness, and at the beginning of light; that is why it has been said that the condition of man is the end of the night and the beginning of day, meaning that he is the sum of all the degrees of imperfection, and that he possesses the degrees of perfection. He has the animal side as well as the angelic side, and the aim of an educator is to so train human souls that their angelic aspect may overcome their animal side. Then if the divine power in man, which is his essential perfection, overcomes the satanic power, which is absolute imperfection, he becomes the most excellent among the creatures; but if the satanic power overcomes the divine power, he becomes the lowest of the creatures. That is why he is the end of imperfection and the beginning of perfection. Not in any other of the species in the world of existence is there such a difference, contrast, contradiction and opposition as in the species of man.[4]

The ever-present tension existing in the human reality is well summed up by these words 'contrast, contradiction and opposition'.

The struggle for existence

The phrase 'struggle for existence' is often used in literature to explain a principle that operates in the world of nature. Its outcome can be seen in the animal kingdom, where a constant fight for survival is going on, where only the strong individuals survive, weak specimens fall victim to predators and no allowance is made for the sick or injured.

One of the consequences of human society turning away from God is that it, too, reverts back to the imperfect conditions of the animal world, and can reflect the kind of behaviour manifested by animals in their natural struggle for existence. 'Abdu'l-Bahá said of this 'inhuman' behaviour:

> This matter of the struggle for existence is the fountain-head of all calamities and is the supreme affliction.[5]

And again He said,

> It is evident, therefore, that the world of nature unassisted is imperfect because it is a plane upon which the struggle for physical existence expresses itself.[6]

> For a period of 6,000 years history informs us about the world of humanity. During these 6,000 years the world of humanity has not been free from war, strife, murder and bloodthirstiness. In every period war has been waged in one country or another and that war was due to either religious prejudice, racial prejudice, political prejudice or patriotic prejudice. It has therefore been ascertained and proved that all prejudices are destructive of the human edifice. As long as these prejudices persist, the struggle for existence must remain dominant . . .[7]

'Abdu'l-Bahá records that the peoples in the East during the 19th century, having turned away from God, were in this condition.

> They were indeed gloomy and dark, negligent of God and under the subjection of the baser instincts and passions of mankind. The struggle for existence was intense and universal.[8]

Even today, the majority of people are susceptible to being caught up in this 'struggle for existence'; apart from a few, they remain 'captives of the world of nature':

> Today, all the peoples of the world are indulging in self-interest and exert the utmost effort and endeavour to promote their own material interests. They are worshipping themselves and not the divine reality, nor the world of mankind. They seek diligently their own benefit and

not the common weal. This is because they are captives of the world of nature and unaware of the divine teachings, of the bounty of the Kingdom and of the Sun of Truth.[9]

The few '. . . who have been freed from the chains and fetters of the material world and, like unto swift-flying birds, are soaring in this unbounded realm' have different desires:

> They are awake and vigilant, they shun the obscurity of the world of nature, their highest wish centereth on the eradication from among men of the struggle for existence, the shining forth of the spirituality and the love of the realm on high, the exercise of utmost kindness among peoples, the realization of an intimate and close connection between religions and the practice of the ideal of self-sacrifice. Then will the world of humanity be transformed into the Kingdom of God.[10]

The ideal power

It is the power which comes through the teachings of the Prophets of God that enables man to rise above this animal-like behaviour and the imperfections of the world of nature.

> And among the teachings of Bahá'u'lláh is man's freedom, that through the ideal Power he should be free and emancipated from the captivity of the world of nature; for as long as man is captive to nature he is a ferocious animal, as the struggle for existence is one of the exigencies of the world of nature.[11]

> Through the breaths of the Holy Spirit it performs miracles; the Orient and the Occident embrace each other, the North and South become intimates and associates, conflicting and contending opinions disappear, antagonistic aims are brushed aside, the law of the struggle for existence is abrogated, and the canopy of the oneness of the world of humanity is raised on the apex of the globe, casting its shade over all the races of men.[12]

The Prophets admonish the peoples of the world, calling on them to leave behind the kinds of behaviour that arise out of the selfish struggle for existence and to express, instead, the virtues arising from the higher nature of man.

> Be generous in prosperity, and thankful in adversity. Be worthy of the trust of thy neighbour, and look upon him with a bright and friendly face. Be a treasure to the poor, an admonisher to the rich, an answerer to the cry of the needy, a preserver of the sanctity of thy pledge. Be fair in thy judgment, and guarded in thy speech. Be unjust to no man, and show all meekness to all men. Be as a lamp unto them that walk in darkness, a joy to the sorrowful, a sea for the thirsty, a haven for the distressed, an upholder and defender of the victim of oppression. Let integrity and uprightness distinguish all thine acts. Be a home for the stranger, a balm to the suffering, a tower of strength for the fugitive. Be eyes to the blind, and a guiding light unto the feet of the erring. Be an ornament to the countenance of truth, a crown to the brow of fidelity, a pillar of the temple of righteousness, a breath of life to the body of mankind, an ensign of the hosts of justice, a luminary above the horizon of virtue, a dew to the soil of the human heart, an ark on the ocean of knowledge, a sun in the heaven of bounty, a gem on the diadem of wisdom, a shining light in the firmament of thy generation, a fruit upon the tree of humility.[13]

One must see in every human being only that which is worthy of praise. When this is done, one can be a friend to the whole human race. If, however, we look at people from the standpoint of their faults, then being a friend to them is a formidable task.[14]

Physical man is temporary

The body is the physical or animal degree of man. From the bodily point of view man is the sharer of the animal kingdom. The bodies alike of men and animals are composed of elements held together by the law of attraction.

Like the animal, man possesses the faculties of the senses, is subject to heat, cold, hunger, thirst, etc.; unlike the animal, man has a rational soul, the human intelligence.[15]

In spite of the fact that the physical body is temporary, being just a composition of elements which will eventually decompose – most people see and accept their physical selves with greater certainty than their spiritual realities which *are* essential and therefore eternal.

> The whole physical creation is perishable. These material bodies are composed of atoms; when these atoms begin to separate decomposition sets in, then comes what we call death. This composition of atoms, which constitutes the body or mortal element of any created being, is temporary. When the power of attraction, which holds these atoms together, is withdrawn, the body, as such, ceases to exist.[16]

The spiritual principle of relativity

Every process unfolding in the world has some spiritual significance, and every action has a spiritual consequence, but not everyone sees life in this way. No explanation will satisfy those who deny the existence of God. Hearts and minds that are closed off to spiritual truths have no insight into the life of the spirit. 'The comprehension of that other life depends on our spiritual birth!' said 'Abdu'l-Bahá.[17]

If asked the question 'What is more "real", spiritual phenomena or physical phenomena?', most people would no doubt reply that the physical world is more 'real' and this observation would be based on their experience of the outward senses of touch, taste, sight, hearing and smell. The surprising truth that emerges from the Bahá'í Writings is that from the spiritual perspective the only things that have any reality at all are associated with the spiritual worlds of God; the physical creation is merely 'the reflection' of the spiritual reality. That is not to say that the physical world about us does not have *any* reality:

> . . . even though absolute being can be attributed only to God we cannot say that other objects have no being. A table has an existence even though its existence compared with the existence of the carpenter who is its maker is almost nothing. Compared to God nothing has existence but this does not mean that even stones do not have being. It is speaking relatively. Moreover, God reveals Himself in all things in the sense that He is the Source of their being and the Cause of their existence.[18]

It is a matter of *relativity* – in *relation* to the spiritual world, the physical has little importance.

> The spiritual world is so much greater than the physical that in comparison with it the physical world is non-existent.[19]

Similar statements can be found in the Qur'án:

> This present life is no other than a pastime and a disport: but truly the future mansion is life indeed![20]

> They rejoice in the life that now is, but this present life is but a passing good, in respect of the life to come![21]

Relationship between the soul and the body

Without the soul, the body of man would be of no consequence:

> The soul of man is the sun by which his body is illumined, and from which it draweth its sustenance, and should be so regarded.[22]

The association of the soul with the physical body is limited to the span of this earthly life. After the death of the body the soul continues, but from that point onwards its existence is purely spiritual.

One of the clearest descriptions contained in the Writings regarding the relationship between the soul and the body is contained in the following passage:

> ... the rational soul, meaning the human spirit, does not descend into the body – that is to say, it does not enter it, for descent and entrance are characteristics of bodies, and the rational soul is exempt from this. The spirit never entered this body, so in quitting it, it will not be in need of an abiding-place; no, the spirit is connected with the body, as this light is with this mirror. When the mirror is clear and perfect, the light of the lamp will be apparent in it, and when the mirror becomes covered with dust or breaks, the light will disappear.[23]

What is more important – body or soul?

On the face of it, this does not seem a sensible question, since clearly a human being is human because he/she has both a body and a soul. However, the reality is that, while the body needs the soul to exist, the soul does not need the body.

> The spirit does not need a body, but the body needs spirit, or it cannot live. The soul can live without a body, but the body without a soul dies.[24]

Therefore it is possible to state quite confidently that the soul is more important than the body. That does not mean that the body should not be properly looked after – of course it should; it is after all the vehicle of the soul, the temple through which the spirit of man expresses itself. However, since the soul continues on after the body has disintegrated, the development of the soul should be man's primary concern.

> We must strive unceasingly and without rest to accomplish the development of the spiritual nature in man, and endeavour with tireless energy to advance humanity toward the nobility of its true and intended station. For the body of man is accidental; it is of no importance. The time of its disintegration will inevitably come. But the spirit of man is essential and, therefore, eternal. It is a divine bounty. It is the effulgence of the Sun of Reality and, therefore, of greater importance than the physical body.[25]

The soul is not a part of the physical creation

The soul is an emanation from the worlds of God. Unlike the physical universe around us, its reality cannot be understood by applying the accepted scientific methods of testing and discovery.

> The soul is not a combination of elements, it is not composed of many atoms, it is of one indivisible substance and therefore eternal. It is entirely out of the order of the physical creation; it is immortal![26]

> Verily I say, the human soul is, in its essence, one of the signs of God, a mystery among His mysteries. It is one of the mighty signs of the

Almighty, the harbinger that proclaimeth the reality of all the worlds of God. Within it lieth concealed that which the world is now utterly incapable of apprehending.[27]

The soul enables a connection with another reality, another dimension apart from the surrounding physical world; it relates man to the eternal worlds of God.

> Thou hast asked Me concerning the nature of the soul. Know, verily, that the soul is a sign of God, a heavenly gem whose reality the most learned of men hath failed to grasp, and whose mystery no mind, however acute, can ever hope to unravel. It is the first among all created things to declare the excellence of its Creator, the first to recognize His glory, to cleave to His truth, and to bow down in adoration before Him.[28]

The soul cannot be seen and its true essence will remain a mystery; yet the knowledge contained in the Writings provides comparatively abundant insights into its powers.

The soul is an 'emanation' – what does this mean?

The explanations contained in the following excerpts are analogies taken from the physical universe which give insight into the meaning of the term 'emanation' as it relates to the nature of the soul.

> Now the writing emanates from the writer, and the discourse emanates from the speaker, and in the same way the human spirit emanates from God.[29]

> Therefore, the proceeding of the human spirits from God is through emanation. When it is said in the Bible that God breathed His spirit into man, this spirit is that which, like the discourse, emanates from the Real Speaker, taking effect in the reality of man.[30]

> It can be compared to the sun from which emanates the light which pours forth on all the creatures; but the sun remains in the exaltation of its sanctity. It does not descend, and it does not resolve itself into luminous forms . . .[31]

Origin of the soul

The Writings explain that the beginning of the human soul coincides with the beginning of the human body, at which time their association is established.

> The soul of man comes into being at conception.[32]

All things which are 'created', which 'come into being' or have a beginning are referred to in the Writings as 'phenomenal', and normally all phenomenal things eventually disappear; they disintegrate or decompose because they are made up of elements which are subject to the forces of nature. The soul is the exception. Although it is referred to by 'Abdu'l-Bahá as phenomenal, it remains unaffected by those material forces of nature because it is an emanation from the spiritual worlds of God; it is not made up of elements, or of anything which can be seen or measured. It has a beginning, but it does not end. The following is part of an explanation of this by 'Abdu'l-Bahá:

> As it is a divine sign, when once it has come into existence, it is eternal. The spirit of man has a beginning, but it has no end; it continues eternally. In the same way the species existing on this earth are phenomenal, for it is established that there was a time when these species did not exist on the surface of the earth. Moreover, the earth has not always existed, but the world of existence has always been, for the universe is not limited to this terrestrial globe. The meaning of this is that, although human souls are phenomenal, they are nevertheless immortal, everlasting and perpetual . . .[33]

Trees grow out of the soil, eventually die and return to the soil. Even the human body, which grows and develops on the earth, will eventually die and decompose, but the soul, because it came from the spiritual worlds of God, will return there after the death of the body and continue on. The fact that the soul is eternal is impossible to comprehend since man can only measure things according to the laws governing the physical world. Time and space do not exist in the spiritual worlds of God, and the soul, being an 'essential' reality, cannot be defined by them. Therefore, once the soul has come into being, its age is irrelevant; a soul is forever.

Words such as eternal, immortal, perpetual, and so on, will remain, at best, intellectual concepts only; our understanding of them limited by the conditions of this physical existence.

> . . . while there is no harm in speculation on these abstract matters, one should not attach too much importance to them. Science itself is far from having resolved the question of the nature of matter, and we cannot, in this physical world, grasp the spiritual one more than in a very fragmentary and inadequate manner.[34]

> This confession of helplessness which mature contemplation must eventually impel every mind to make is in itself the acme of human understanding, and marketh the culmination of man's development.[35]

Evolution of the species toward spiritual capacity

Greatness always existed (potentially) in man, however the capability to express spiritual perfections and qualities was acquired only gradually; this was the outcome of a long process of evolution, including physical evolution. The Bahá'í view of evolution indicates that all species including man were created complete from the first, and although they may have changed form, they never lost their unique identity, having all gone through a gradual process of growth and development before reaching the limit of their physical perfections.

Similarly, in the spiritual sense, *evolution* is used to describe the gradual realization within the human species of the great potential latent in it and which has always existed.

> In the world of existence man has traversed successive degrees until he has attained the human kingdom. In each degree of his progression he has developed capacity for advancement to the next station and condition. While in the kingdom of the mineral he was attaining the capacity for promotion into the degree of the vegetable. In the kingdom of the vegetable he underwent preparation for the world of the animal, and from thence he has come onward to the human degree, or kingdom. Throughout this journey of progression he has ever and always been potentially man.[36]

Therefore, this change of appearance, this evolution of members, this development and growth, even though we admit the reality of growth and progress, does not prevent the species from being original. Man from the beginning was in this perfect form and composition, and possessed capacity and aptitude for acquiring material and spiritual perfections . . .[37]

So also the formation of man in the matrix of the world was in the beginning like the embryo; then gradually he made progress in perfectness, and grew and developed until he reached the state of maturity, when the mind and spirit became visible in the greatest power. In the beginning of his formation the mind and spirit also existed, but they were hidden; later they were manifested. In the womb of the world mind and spirit also existed in the embryo, but they were concealed; afterward they appeared. So it is that in the seed the tree exists, but it is hidden and concealed; when it develops and grows, the complete tree appears. In the same way the growth and development of all beings is gradual; this is the universal divine organization and the natural system. The seed does not at once become a tree; the embryo does not at once become a man; the mineral does not suddenly become a stone. No, they grow and develop gradually and attain the limit of perfection.

All beings, whether large or small, were created perfect and complete from the first, but their perfections appear in them by degrees. The organization of God is one; the evolution of existence is one; the divine system is one. Whether they be small or great beings, all are subject to one law and system.[38]

Realizing this we may acknowledge the fact that at one time man was an inmate of the sea, at another period an invertebrate, then a vertebrate and finally a human being standing erect. Though we admit these changes, we cannot say man is an animal. In each one of these stages are signs and evidences of his human existence and destination. Proof of this lies in the fact that in the embryo man still resembles a worm. This embryo still progresses from one state to another, assuming different forms until that which was potential in it – namely, the human image – appears. Therefore, in the protoplasm, man is man. Conservation of species demands it.

The lost link of Darwinian theory is itself a proof that man is not an animal. How is it possible to have all the links present and that important link absent? Its absence is an indication that man has never been an animal. It will never be found.[39]

Then man became capable

Finally that point was reached when it became possible for the human species to receive spiritual teachings from the Messengers of God.

> Similarly, in the contingent world, the human species hath undergone progressive physical changes and, by a slow process, hath scaled the ladder of civilization, realizing in itself the wonders, excellencies and gifts of humanity in their most glorious form, until it gained the capacity to express the splendours of spiritual perfections and divine ideals and became capable of hearkening to the call of God. Then at last the call of the Kingdom was raised, the spiritual virtues and perfections were revealed, the Sun of Reality dawned, and the teachings of the Most Great Peace, of the oneness of the world of humanity and of the universality of men, were promoted.[40]

Since acquiring the capacity to know of its creator, humanity has progressed, both materially and spiritually, through a 'vast and irresistible process'[41] stimulated by the appearance of the Prophets of God.

The mystical link between the soul and its Creator

The climax of this process of evolution is the awakening of man, the realization that our essential reality is spiritual and not physical, the acceptance of the truth that 'man is in reality, a spiritual being . . .'[42]

This world is not the true home of the soul; in a sense souls are 'out of place' in this physical environment and are destined to return to the spiritual worlds from which they came.

> All men have proceeded from God and unto Him shall all return.[43]

This rational soul, the 'sign' of God, having become associated with the human body at the point of conception, traverses this physical world for a time and then continues on into a new, spiritual existence. Like a unique fragment of an unknown and unknowable 'other Reality', the soul yearns to return to the source of its genesis, to be reunited with the force which first propelled it on a journey . . . a journey of testing during which it can gather to itself tremendous power through the discovery of the great spiritual forces latent within it.

The nature of this mystical connection between the human soul and the Creator is referred to in various ways by Bahá'u'lláh in the *Hidden Words;* for example He says:

> Thou art My lamp and My light is in thee.[44]

> . . . within thee have I placed the essence of My light . . . [45]

> My love is in thee, know it, that thou mayest find Me near unto thee.[46]

The power of attraction

> It is so, likewise, in the spiritual world. That world is the Kingdom of complete attraction and affinity.[47]

The great search to find meaning in life and to discover the reality of things arises from this inbuilt spiritual attraction the soul has to its Creator. This power of attraction has been imprinted on our souls; it is part of us. Whether people are conscious of it or not, this power of attraction gives birth to our inner condition of spiritual need, the desire to understand the purpose of life, to know of the creative power behind all existence.

'Abdu'l-Bahá states that the mind of man is drawn to intellectual investigation and scientific discovery because 'God has created or deposited this love of reality in man'.[48] Similarly, the soul is drawn towards spiritual discovery because God has created man for that purpose.

In the *Hidden Words* we read:

> O Son of Spirit! My claim on thee is great, it cannot be forgotten. My grace to thee is plenteous, it cannot be veiled. My love has made in thee its home, it cannot be concealed. My light is manifest to thee, it cannot be obscured.[49]

When the heart is no longer attached to the material world and, instead, becomes inspired with the love of God, then the soul will come under the influence of what 'Abdu'l-Bahá referred to as 'the divine force of magnetism'. In the following mystical passage, His description of magnetism elevates it to a sublime position well beyond man's experience of it in this world:

> . . . any movement animated by love moveth from the periphery to the centre, from space to the Day-Star of the universe. Perchance thou deemest this to be difficult, but I tell thee that such cannot be the case, for when the motivating and guiding power is the divine force of magnetism it is possible, by its aid, to traverse time and space easily and swiftly.[50]

The lover's desire is to find the loved one – nothing else will satisfy

The soul, which emanated from God, yearns to know its Creator. Acquiring the knowledge of God is the only possible means to satisfy that yearning.

> O Son of Utterance! Turn thy face unto Mine and renounce all save Me; for My sovereignty endureth and My dominion perisheth not. If thou seekest another than Me, yea, if thou searchest the universe for evermore, thy quest will be in vain.[51]

> O Son of Man! Be thou content with Me and seek no other helper. For none but Me can ever suffice thee.[52]

When the soul, which is the sign of God in this world, acknowledges its Creator and experiences the love of God, it becomes spiritually awakened, and that awakening leads to questioning:

'What is the nature of my reality, my true self?'

'Why am I here?'

The best possible outcome of this awakening is that the soul acquires the knowledge of the Messenger of God, becomes attached to Him and is transformed by reading the Word of God. This is how the spirit of faith is born, and the soul begins (through tests faced and overcome) to acquire the attributes which will prepare it for entrance into the spiritual worlds of God. This process fulfils the purpose for which man was created.

While this may sound straightforward, people have such a strong attachment to the things of this world that this effectively veils them from the light of knowledge. Therefore, the central challenge of this life is to remove those veils which keep our souls from becoming illumined.

However, before moving on to examine the subject of spiritual 'veils' and their relationship to the physical world, it is important to look at the subject of 'light', and how central it is to having an adequate understanding of spiritual matters.

CHAPTER 4

WORLDS OF LIGHT

And the light shineth in darkness; and the darkness comprehended it not.
John 1:5

There are numerous references to 'light' in the Holy Books of the Prophets of God, but for the purposes of this book, this chapter will examine a selection of passages that reveal how this divine attribute manifests itself and how the word 'light' is used to convey spiritual concepts.

Material light and spiritual light

First, what is the difference between light as we understand it in this world and the 'spiritual light' referred to in the Word of God?

> The light is divided into two kinds, material and spiritual. The material light is a vanishing matter and is known by etheric vibrations. But the spiritual light is the divine, eternal and never-ending quality and is a truth of the Kingdom.[1]

Material light is a phenomenon of this world of existence, whereas spiritual light is a divine attribute which illumines all the worlds of God. In a number of the excerpts that follow in this chapter, the spiritual worlds are described in terms of light.

Other worlds

References to other worlds apart from this physical world are contained in the writings of all the Messengers of God. There are many references to 'the next world' in the Qur'án, and the Bible contains Christ's promise to His disciples: 'In My Father's house are many mansions . . .'[2]

The Bahá'í Writings, also, contain a number of remarkable statements on the subject of the worlds of God. Take for example the following excerpt:

> As to thy question concerning the worlds of God. Know thou of a truth that the worlds of God are countless in their number, and infinite in their range. None can reckon or comprehend them except God, the All-Knowing, the All-Wise.[3]

Worlds of light

Beyond the material world are worlds of light:

> But praise be to God, the world of existence does not culminate here. If this were so, existence itself would be sterile. There are many worlds of light. For even as the plant imagines life ends with itself and has no knowledge of our existence, so the materially-minded man has no knowledge of other worlds of consciousness.[4]

In the Writings there are many instances in the written memorials extolling the lives of some of the early believers where the next world is referred to as being a world of light. For example:

> Finally . . . he left this darksome, narrow world and hastened away to the land of lights.[5]

Other phrases used are: 'submerged in an ocean of lights';[6] 'he finally departed to eternal light';[7] 'May they be immersed in tiers of light';[8] '. . . in the Kingdom of Lights';[9] 'hath hastened to the sanctified realm of light'.[10] The following excerpt from a prayer is particularly beautiful:

> O Lord, glorify his station, shelter him under the pavilion of Thy supreme mercy, cause him to enter Thy glorious paradise, and perpetuate his existence in Thine exalted rose garden, that he may plunge into the sea of light in the world of mysteries.[11]

Even the physical resting-places of these exemplary persons are associated with this heavenly light: 'Holy be her dust, as the tiers of light come down on it from Heaven';[12] 'May his grave be encircled with lights . . .';[13] '[may God] . . . cause to descend there range on range of light';[14] 'May God light up his resting-place . . .';[15] 'I beg of God to cause spheres of light to descend upon thy sepulchre.'[16]

Light and the influence of souls in the next world

The Light of God is like the sun and the soul of man is like the mirror; that is the analogy used to describe this relationship. Souls who acquire spiritual qualities while in this world continue to reflect the light of God after their passing, and their spiritual radiance is such that they unfailingly exert a beneficial influence upon this world of existence. One particular passage refers to this as 'the light of guidance that cometh from the Company on high'.[17]

The purer the soul (i.e. the cleaner the mirror), the greater its capacity will be to reflect that light and, hence, the greater its influence.

> Souls are like unto mirrors, and the bounty of God is like unto the sun. When the mirrors pass beyond all colouring and attain purity and polish, and are confronted with the sun, they will reflect in full perfection its light and glory.[18]

The following quotation reveals how those illumined souls in the next world influence this world:

> The light which these souls radiate is responsible for the progress of the world and the advancement of its peoples. They are like unto leaven which leaveneth the world of being, and constitute the animating force through which the arts and wonders of the world are made manifest. Through them the clouds rain their bounty upon men, and the earth bringeth forth its fruits. All things must needs have a cause, a motive power, an animating principle. These souls and symbols of detachment have provided, and will continue to provide, the supreme moving impulse in the world of being.[19]

It is evident from this statement that while death of the physical body brings about a change in condition, the soul does not suddenly cease activity – 'work' goes on.

Those who have passed on through death, have a sphere of their own. It is not removed from ours; their work, the work of the Kingdom, is ours; but it is sanctified from what we call 'time and place'. Time with us is measured by the sun. When there is no more sunrise, and no more sunset, that kind of time does not exist for man.[20]

Eternal light

Opening our physical eyes enables us to look at the physical world around us; similarly, opening 'the conscious eye of the soul' makes man aware of the existence of 'eternal light'.

> The bestowals of God which are manifest in all phenomenal life are sometimes hidden by intervening veils of mental and mortal vision which render man spiritually blind and incapable, but when those scales are removed and the veils rent asunder, then the great signs of God will become visible, and he will witness the eternal light filling the world.[21]

For those who think of 'spiritual light' as not 'sensible' (that is, not able to be perceived by the senses) and doubt that such a thing exists, 'Abdu'l-Bahá points to magnetism and to so-called visible light – both of which are evidently not 'sensible' – to show that the existence of *those* energies is not disputed.

> If we wish to deny everything that is not sensible, then we must deny the realities which unquestionably exist. For example, ethereal matter is not sensible, though it has an undoubted existence. The power of attraction is not sensible, though it certainly exists. From what do we affirm these existences? From their signs. Thus this light is the vibration of that ethereal matter, and from this vibration we infer the existence of ether.[22]

Although heavenly or 'eternal' light cannot be detected by the outward senses, man has the capacity to become aware of it through the power of 'inner vision' or 'insight' which is a faculty of the soul.

> As to the light thou dost witness: It is not an earthly light (phenomenal); nay, rather, it is a heavenly light. It cannot be seen by the sight; nay, rather, it is perceived by the insight.[23]

Like the human soul, this spiritual light emanates from the worlds of God; its existence is closely connected with the development of the soul, because once illumined by this light, the soul will begin to acquire the powers and qualities necessary for its continuing journey beyond this world.

Light of the love of God

Another term used in the Writings to convey the concept of spiritual light is 'the love of God': 'Love gives life to the lifeless. Love lights a flame in the heart that is cold. Love brings hope to the hopeless and gladdens the hearts of the sorrowful.'[24]

The light of love has a transforming effect upon those who love God, and this is evident in their faces. It causes them to radiate happiness and it illumines them in a way unrelated to physical illumination. While perhaps not recognizing what it is, the seeker will be attracted to this spiritual radiance which shines out from them.

> In thy face a brilliant light is apparent and that sparkling light is the love of God. All faces are dark except the face which is a mirror of the light of the love of divinity. This light is not accidental – it is eternal. It is not temporal but real. When the heart hath become clear and pure then the face will become illuminated, because the face is the mirror of the heart.[25]

Note these descriptions of people who reflected the light of the love of God:

> What a radiant face he had! He was nothing but light from head to foot. Just to look at that face made one happy; he was so confident, so assured, so rooted in his faith, and his expression so joyous.[26]

> He was a man amazing to behold, his face so luminous that even those who were not believers used to say that a heavenly light shone from his forehead.[27]

These observations point to the transfiguring effect which such love has on the eyes, the face and the countenance of those who become illumined by its light, and show that this is readily recognized by others in spite of the fact that it is an entirely spiritual effect.

In many of His prayers 'Abdu'l-Bahá refers to this light of the love of God. For example:

> O Lord, brighten Thou my face with the lights of Thy bestowals, light Thou mine eyes with beholding the signs of Thine all-subduing might; delight my heart with the glory of Thy knowledge that encompasseth all things, gladden Thou my soul with Thy soul-reviving tidings of great joy, O Thou King of this world and the Kingdom above . . .[28]

Light of the attributes of God

> Hence we can observe the traces and attributes of God, which are resplendent in all phenomena and shining as the sun at midday, and know surely that these emanate from an infinite source.[29]

One thing that soon becomes apparent when reading the Writings is that mention of any of the spiritual attributes is often associated with light. For example, there are references to the light of *tolerance and righteousness*, the lights of *intellect and wisdom*, the light of *knowledge*, the light of *unity*, the light of *honesty*, the light of *justice*, the light of *certitude*, the light of *mercy*, the light of *assurance*, the light of *tenderness*, the light of *certainty*, the light of a *good character*, the light of *piety and uprightness*, the light of *detachment*, the light of *courtesy*, the light of *long-suffering*, the light of *liberty*, the light of *sanctity and purity*, the light of *faithfulness*, the lights of *mercy and beneficence*, the light of *truth*, and the light of *trust and detachment*.

In one instance, mention of '*trustworthiness*' is accompanied by a mystical description and a statement about the influence that this attribute has upon the world:

> Turning, then, to the left We gazed on one of the Beauties of the Most Sublime Paradise, standing on a pillar of light, and calling aloud saying: 'O inmates of earth and heaven! Behold ye My beauty, and My radiance, and My revelation, and My effulgence. By God, the True One! I am Trustworthiness and the revelation thereof, and the beauty thereof. I will recompense whosoever will cleave unto Me, and recognize My rank and station, and hold fast unto My hem. I am the most great ornament of the people of Bahá, and the vesture of glory unto all who are in the kingdom of creation. I am the supreme instrument

for the prosperity of the world, and the horizon of assurance unto all beings.'[30]

Light of the Names of God

Similarly, references to some of the Names of God are preceded by the words *'the light of'*, and certain passages reveal the effects which the light of these Names have upon the world:

> It should be borne in mind, however, that when the light of My Name, *the All-Pervading*, hath shed its radiance upon the universe, each and every created thing hath, according to a fixed decree, been endowed with the capacity to exercise a particular influence, and been made to possess a distinct virtue . . .
>
> Consider, for instance, the revelation of the light of the Name of God, *the Educator*. Behold, how in all things the evidences of such a revelation are manifest, how the betterment of all beings dependeth upon it.[31]

> Consider, in like manner, the revelation of the light of the Name of God, *the Incomparable*. Behold, how this light hath enveloped the entire creation, how each and every thing manifesteth the sign of His Unity, testifieth to the reality of Him Who is the Eternal Truth, proclaimeth His sovereignty, His oneness, and His power. This revelation is a token of His mercy that hath encompassed all created things.[32]

These Writings reveal that the attributes of God the Creator are evident in everything; they are the cause of the illumination of the world.

> Say: Nature in its essence is the embodiment of My Name, *the Maker, the Creator*. Its manifestations are diversified by varying causes, and in this diversity there are signs for men of discernment. Nature is God's Will and is its expression in and through the contingent world. It is a dispensation of Providence ordained by the Ordainer, the All-Wise. Were anyone to affirm that it is the Will of God as manifested in the world of being, no one should question this assertion. It is endowed with a power whose reality men of learning fail to grasp. Indeed a man of insight can perceive naught therein save the effulgent splendour of Our Name, the Creator. Say: This is an existence which knoweth no decay, and Nature

> itself is lost in bewilderment before its revelations, its compelling evidences and its effulgent glory which have encompassed the universe.[33]

> Nay, were man to gaze with the eye of divine and spiritual discernment, he will readily recognize that nothing whatsoever can exist without the revelation of the splendour of God, the ideal King. Consider how all created things eloquently testify to the revelation of that inner Light within them.[34]

Light of the Messengers of God

The divine Messengers are the channels of God's love and their appearance is the cause of an outpouring of spiritual radiance in the world.

> And when He purposed to manifest His beauty in the kingdom of names and to reveal His glory in the realm of attributes, He brought forth His Prophets from the invisible plane to the visible, that His name 'the Manifest' might be distinguished from 'the Hidden' . . .[35]

> From each and every revelation emanating from the Source of His glory, holy and never-ending evidences of unimaginable splendour have appeared, and out of every manifestation of His invincible power oceans of eternal light have outpoured.[36]

It is as if a kind father has made provision for the care and education of his children in order that they may grow and develop into an ideal state of maturity.

> The people are in darkness; the Prophets bring them into the realm of light. They are in a state of utter imperfection; the Prophets imbue them with perfections. The purpose of the prophetic mission is none other than the education and guidance of the people.[37]

Abraham, Moses and Christ

Again, in the following references to Abraham, Moses and Christ, their appearances in the world are associated with light:

> Later, the beauty of the countenance of the Friend of God appeared from behind the veil, and another standard of divine guidance was hoisted. He invited the people of the earth to the light of righteousness.[38]
>
> And when His day was ended, there came the turn of Moses . . . He shone forth from the Sinai of light upon the world. He summoned all the peoples and kindreds of the earth to the kingdom of eternity, and invited them to partake of the fruit of the tree of faithfulness.[39]
>
> And when the days of Moses were ended, and the light of Jesus, shining forth from the dayspring of the Spirit, encompassed the world, all the people of Israel arose in protest against Him.[40]

All the Messengers of God have shone the light of God's love upon humanity according to the needs of each age in which They appeared.

> All the Prophets are lights, they only differ in degree; they shine like brilliant heavenly bodies, each have their appointed place and time of ascension. Some are like lamps, some like the moon, some like distant stars, and a few are like the sun, shining from one end of the earth to the other. All have the same Light to give, yet they are different in degree.[41]
>
> It hath, therefore, become manifest and evident that within the tabernacles of these Prophets and chosen Ones of God the light of His infinite names and exalted attributes hath been reflected . . .[42]

In this day a new episode in the spiritual life of humanity has begun and the light of God's love has once again shone down upon humanity.

Lovers of the light

'Abdu'l-Bahá uses the analogies of the lamp and the light, and then the sun and its dawning-point, to explain the essential oneness of the teachings of the Prophets of God. He urges man to become a lover of the light, not a worshipper of lamps. Here are a few of His clear explanations of this essential principle underlying the religion of God:

> A Divine Manifestation is as a mirror reflecting the light of the Sun. The

light is the same and yet the mirror is not the Sun. All the Manifestations of God bring the same Light; they only differ in degree, not in reality. The Truth is one. The light is the same though the lamps may be different; we must look at the Light not at the Lamp. If we accept the Light in one, we must accept the Light in all; all agree, because all are the same. The teaching is ever the same, it is only the outward forms that change.[43]

Likewise the divine religions of the holy Manifestations of God are in reality one, though in name and nomenclature they differ. Man must be a lover of the light, no matter from what dayspring it may appear. He must be a lover of the rose, no matter in what soil it may be growing. He must be a seeker of the truth, no matter from what source it come. Attachment to the lantern is not loving the light.[44]

If the sun were to rise in the West, it would still be the sun; one must not withdraw from it on account of its rising-place, nor consider the West to be always the place of sunset. In the same way, one must look for the heavenly bounties and seek for the Divine Aurora. In every place where it appears, one must become its distracted lover. Consider that if the Jews had not kept turning to the horizon of Moses, and had only regarded the Sun of Reality, without any doubt they would have recognized the Sun in the dawning-place of the reality of Christ, in the greatest divine splendour. But, alas! a thousand times alas! attaching themselves to the outward words of Moses, they were deprived of the divine bounties and the lordly splendours![45]

In order to become lovers of the light, it is necessary to detach ourselves from the kingdom of names.

If we are lovers of the light, we adore it in whatever lamp it may become manifest, but if we love the lamp itself and the light is transferred to another lamp, we will neither accept nor sanction it. Therefore, we must follow and adore the virtues revealed in the Messengers of God – whether in Abraham, Moses, Jesus or other Prophets – but we must not adhere to and adore the lamp. We must recognize the sun, no matter from what dawning point it may shine forth, be it Mosaic, Abrahamic or any personal point of orientation whatever, for we are lovers of sunlight and not of orientation. We are lovers of illumination and not of lamps and candles. We are seekers for water, no matter from what rock it may gush forth. We are in need of fruit in whatsoever orchard it may be ripened. We long for rain; it matters not which cloud pours it down.[46]

Light . . . upon the reality of man

Reading the above quotations should help in contemplating the following most remarkable passages from the Writings of Bahá'u'lláh.

> The supreme cause for creating the world and all that is therein is for man to know God.[47]

> Upon the inmost reality of each and every created thing He hath shed the light of one of His names, and made it a recipient of the glory of one of His attributes. Upon the reality of man, however, He hath focused the radiance of all of His names and attributes, and made it a mirror of His own Self. Alone of all created things man hath been singled out for so great a favour, so enduring a bounty.[48]

> Whatever is in the heavens and whatever is on the earth is a direct evidence of the revelation within it of the attributes and names of God, inasmuch as within every atom are enshrined the signs that bear eloquent testimony to the revelation of that Most Great Light. Methinks, but for the potency of that revelation, no being could ever exist. How resplendent the luminaries of knowledge that shine in an atom, and how vast the oceans of wisdom that surge within a drop! To a supreme degree is this true of man, who, among all created things, hath been invested with the robe of such gifts, and hath been singled out for the glory of such distinction. For in him are potentially revealed all the attributes and names of God to a degree that no other created being hath excelled or surpassed. All these names and attributes are applicable to him. Even as He hath said: 'Man is My mystery, and I am his mystery.'[49]

Souls are depositories of the light of God

> Hence we can observe the traces and attributes of God, which are resplendent in all phenomena and shining as the sun at midday, and know surely that these emanate from an infinite source.[50]

Although the traces of God can be seen in all things, the excerpts quoted above show that in man these divine attributes are 'potentially revealed' to the highest degree. The human soul is a depository. Therefore, in order to know ourselves we must come to understand the nature of the spiritual attributes which God has deposited within all of us.

> Just now the soil of human hearts seems like black earth, but in the innermost substance of this dark soil there are thousands of fragrant flowers latent. We must endeavour to cultivate and awaken these potentialities, discover the secret treasure in this very mine and depository of God, bring forth these resplendent powers long hidden in human hearts.[51]

The spiritual reality of man was created from the essence of the divine attributes:

> Out of the essence of knowledge I gave thee being, why seekest thou enlightenment from anyone beside Me? Out of the clay of love I moulded thee, how dost thou busy thyself with another? Turn thy sight unto thyself, that thou mayest find Me standing within thee, mighty, powerful and self-subsisting.[52]

All the names and attributes of God are reflected to some degree in the soul and therefore, by knowing our spiritual selves, we shall know God – not the essence or reality of the Creator, but rather, the power of His signs and attributes.

> The object of God's teaching to man is that man may know himself in order to comprehend the greatness of God.[53]

> Man is said to be the greatest representative of God, and he is the Book of Creation because all the mysteries of beings exist in him.[54]

The Messengers illumine the pathway to God

God through His bounty sends us Divine Messengers, the Manifestations of God; They are perfect mirrors reflecting God's light into this world of being, illumining hearts and revealing spiritual truths. This is why it is said that to come to know the Messengers of God is the same as coming to know God; to love them is to love God.

> The knowledge of the Reality of the Divinity is impossible and unattainable, but the knowledge of the Manifestations of God is the knowledge of God, for the bounties, splendours and divine attributes are apparent in them. Therefore, if man attains to the knowledge of the Manifestations of God, he will attain to the knowledge of God . . .[55]

As Christ said, 'he that hath seen me hath seen the Father . . .'[56]

Whenever a new Messenger appears in the world He tells the people that the *only* pathway to the knowledge of God is through Him. For example, Muhammad stated:

> But whoso shall sever himself from the prophet after that 'the guidance' hath been manifested to him, and shall follow any other path than that of the faithful, we will turn our back on him as he hath turned his back on us . . .[57]

Similarly, Christ said: 'I am the way, the truth, and the life: no man cometh unto the Father, but by me.'[58] That statement of truth remained in effect until the coming of the next divine Messenger, which He Himself foretold. The appearance of a new Messenger of God is a renewal of the light of God, the return of the same divine spirit in a different human form.

Every Messenger of God both fulfils and foretells. He fulfils the prophecies of the previous Messenger regarding the return of the Spirit of God, and in the process of revealing the Word of God again He foretells the coming of the next Messenger. This is the enduring pattern of divine revelation.

Light of the Word of God

In a previous chapter the most potent expression of the Word of God was explored, that is, as the Creative Force and the Cause of all existence. Here, the Word of God is shown to be the source of illumination to the world of humanity:

Likewise, in the spiritual realm of intelligence and idealism there must be a centre of illumination, and that centre is the everlasting, ever-shining Sun, the Word of God. Its lights are the lights of reality which have shone upon humanity, illumining the realm of thought and morals, conferring the bounties of the divine world upon man. These lights are the cause of the education of souls and the source of the enlightenment of hearts, sending forth in effulgent radiance the message of the glad tidings of the Kingdom of God.[59]

Influence of the Word of God on society

Our limited experience of this awesome spiritual power is through the revelation (spoken and written Word of God) associated with each Prophet. Every revelation from God, being an expression of that universal force, has a great beneficial influence upon the world of humanity, carrying forward both the spiritual and material evolution of society. For example:

> Through the Love of God, Christ was sent into the world with His inspiring example of a perfect life of self-sacrifice and devotion, bringing to men the message of Eternal Life. It was the Love of God that gave Muhammad power to bring the Arabs from a state of animal degradation to a loftier state of existence.[60]

At times Bahá'u'lláh refers to the Word of God as the 'City of Certitude' and He explains that this 'City' contains spiritual sustenance, knowledge, guidance, blessings, learning, understanding, faith, and certitude.

For those seeking spiritual knowledge, there is something deeply satisfying about reading the Word of God, perhaps because these words are a tangible link between this world and the next world.

> Such are the mysteries of the Word of God, which have been unveiled and made manifest, that haply thou mayest apprehend the morning light of divine guidance, mayest quench, by the power of reliance and renunciation, the lamp of idle fancy, of vain imaginings, of hesitation, and doubt, and mayest kindle, in the inmost chamber of thine heart, the new-born light of divine knowledge and certitude.[61]

Influence of the Word of God on the individual

The Word of God revives man.

> Every word that proceedeth out of the mouth of God is endowed with such potency as can instill new life into every human frame...[62]

> Through the movement of Our Pen of glory We have, at the bidding of the omnipotent Ordainer, breathed a new life into every human frame, and instilled into every word a fresh potency. All created things proclaim the evidences of this world-wide regeneration.[63]

It is motivating.

> Direct thine attention to the holy Tablets... They are the spirit of life, the ark of salvation, the magnet to draw down eternal glory, the dynamic power to motivate the inner self of man.[64]

It causes the soul to soar.

> Give ear unto the verses of God... They are assuredly the infallible balance, established by God, the Lord of this world and the next. Through them the soul of man is caused to wing its flight towards the Dayspring of Revelation, and the heart of every true believer is suffused with light.[65]

It unfolds the mysteries of God and brings the greatest happiness to the seeker!

> May your souls be illumined by the light of the Words of God, and may you become repositories of the mysteries of God, for no comfort is greater and no happiness is sweeter than spiritual comprehension of the divine teachings.[66]

CHAPTER 5

SPIRITUAL QUICKENING

Springtime in nature witnesses the return of life to the earth; it causes the quickening of living things. Spring has a counterpart in the spiritual world. The periodic appearance of the Messengers of God in the world signals the return of the spiritual springtime, the renewal of spiritual life in man. In one of His Tablets, Bahá'u'lláh lists two of the many Names of God as 'the Raiser from the dead' and 'the Quickener'.[1]

In medical terminology 'quickening' is a word that has been used to describe the moment when the mother first becomes aware of the baby's movements within her womb. In other words, it is the moment of awareness of a new life. In spiritual terminology, 'quickening' relates to the awakening of the soul of man into spiritual life.

> God has sent forth the Prophets for the purpose of quickening the soul of man into higher and divine recognitions. He has revealed the heavenly Books for this great purpose. For this the breaths of the Holy Spirit have been wafted through the gardens of human hearts . . .[2]

God's Messengers awaken man's spiritual nature and stimulate its development. They are the spiritual catalysts to the world of humanity, resuscitating, renewing and inspiring man.

> Even so is the spiritual springtime when it comes. When the holy, divine Manifestations or Prophets appear in the world, a cycle of radiance, an age of mercy dawns. Everything is renewed. Minds, hearts and all human forces are reformed, perfections are quickened, sciences, discoveries and investigations are stimulated afresh, and everything appertaining to the virtues of the human world is revitalized.[3]

> For this reason the holy Manifestations of God appear in the human world. They come to educate and illuminate mankind, to bestow spiritual susceptibilities, to quicken inner perceptions and thereby adorn the reality of man – the human temple – with divine graces.[4]

> He is indeed as one dead who, at the wondrous dawn of this Revelation, hath failed to be quickened by its soul-stirring breeze.[5]

The gift of life is common to all, but 'spiritual life' begins only when the soul is quickened by the breath of the Holy Spirit.

Christ distinguished between physical life and spiritual life in His statement 'That which is born of the flesh is flesh; and that which is born of the Spirit is spirit,'[6] and described those persons devoid of the spirit of faith as being 'dead'. He said, 'Except a man be born again, he cannot see the kingdom of God.'[7]

Muhammad said: 'How can ye withhold faith from God? Ye were dead and He gave you life; next He will cause you to die; next He will restore you to life: next shall ye return to Him!'[8] 'He called us to the faith – "Believe ye on your Lord" – and we have believed.'[9]

The hunger and the thirst

> Draw me nearer unto the river that is life indeed, for my soul burneth with thirst in its ceaseless search after Thee.[10]

> Verily Thy lovers thirst, O my Lord; lead them to the wellspring of bounty and grace. Verily, they hunger; send down unto them Thy heavenly table. Verily, they are naked; robe them in the garments of learning and knowledge.[11]

The hunger and thirst for spiritual life is in man because the soul yearns to know its Creator. Many people search for meaning in their lives to satisfy their spiritual thirst, not understanding what they seek, or why. Consequently, they may search in the wrong place and perhaps spend many years engaged in acquiring knowledge, prosperity, fame or other material things, only to find in the end that they did not quench that thirst.

When the human spirit turns away from its higher nature and denies the existence of God, it focuses its capacity to love on the things of the world, smothering the spiritual susceptibilities. However, nothing in the material world can ever satisfy the heart of man – only the spiritual sustenance contained in the Word of God can quench that yearning.

Referring to the Word of God, Bahá'u'lláh promises that 'the attainment of this City quencheth thirst without water, and kindleth the love of God without fire'.[12] And in one of His revealed prayers are the words 'my remembrance of Thee, O my God, quencheth my thirst, and quieteth my heart'.[13]

The spiritual bread and water

Throughout history the Messengers of God have brought the 'water of life' and the 'food from the heavenly table' to satisfy the spiritual needs of man; these are the symbols of spiritual sustenance which denote the Word of God. These same symbols were used by Christ when He called the people of Israel to the Word of God.

> And Jesus said unto them, I am the bread of life: he that cometh to me shall never hunger; and he that believeth on me shall never thirst.[14]

All those who turn towards God will find God, but not all will show a thirst for the spiritual life.

> The mass of the people are occupied with self and worldly desire, are immersed in the ocean of the nether world and are captives of the world of nature . . .[15]

> The peoples of the world are fast asleep. Were they to wake from their slumber, they would hasten with eagerness unto God, the All-Knowing, the All-Wise. They would cast away everything they possess, be it all the treasures of the earth, that their Lord may remember them to the extent of addressing to them but one word.[16]

The power of attraction

One of the great gifts of God is that through His mercy and bounty He has deposited the spiritual power of attraction in every human soul, deserving or not.

> It is from the bounty of God that man is selected for the highest degree ... For faith, which is life eternal, is the sign of bounty, and not the result of justice. The flame of the fire of love, in this world of earth and water, comes through the power of attraction and not by effort and striving ... only the light of the Divine Beauty can transport and move the spirits through the force of attraction.[17]

Yet it is a power which remains in potential only, until it is activated. When activated, this strong power of attraction between the soul and its Creator leads to recognition of God's Messenger, to belief in Him, and to the spirit of Faith being born in the soul. God, however, does not force man. In this mystical association between God and man, love is the bonding agent, the principle which connects the two parties; it is a relationship based on choice. God can choose:

> Verily, my God chooses whomsoever He willeth, by His mercy and generosity, for entrance into the Kingdom of Glory and shineth the lights of (His) Beauty upon them.[18]

> Verily thy Lord lighteth the lamp of love in the heart of whomsoever He chooseth. This is indeed the great happiness.[19]

> Knowledge is a light which God casteth into the heart of whomsoever He willeth.[20]

And man can choose:

> Blessed is he who hath rent the intervening veils asunder and is illumined by the radiant light of divine Revelation.[21]

> No man that seeketh Us will We ever disappoint, neither shall he that hath set his face towards Us be denied access unto Our court ... .[22]

The bounty of being chosen for the knowledge of God has been referred to in previous revelations. For example, in one of the parables, Christ said, 'For many are called, but few are chosen.'[23] And in the Qur'án, we find Muhammad referring to both parties to this covenant:

> Whom He pleaseth will God choose for it, and whosoever shall turn to Him in penitence will He guide to it.[24]

> . . . for God is surely the guider of those who believe, into the straight path.[25]

Those who receive this gift of spiritual life and have been awakened by that quickening power can consider themselves to be truly favoured.

> But ye . . . are at present especially favoured with this bounty, have become of the chosen, have been informed of the heavenly instructions, have gained admittance into the Kingdom of God, have become the recipients of unbounded blessings and have been baptized with the Water of Life, with the fire of the love of God and with the Holy Spirit.[26]

The value of this gift is inestimable, as many of the revealed prayers testify:

> I render Thee thanks, O Thou Who hast lighted Thy fire within my soul, and cast the beams of Thy light into my heart . . .[27]

> O Thou, my God, Who guidest the seeker to the pathway that leadeth aright, Who deliverest the lost and blinded soul out of the wastes of perdition, Thou Who bestowest upon the sincere great bounties and favours, Who guardest the frightened within Thine impregnable refuge, Who answerest, from Thine all-highest horizon, the cry of those who cry out unto Thee. Praised be Thou, O my Lord! Thou hast guided the distracted out of the death of unbelief, and hast brought those who draw nigh unto Thee to the journey's goal . . .[28]

> My God, my Adored One, my King, my Desire! What tongue can voice my thanks to Thee? I was heedless, Thou didst awaken me. I had turned back from Thee, Thou didst graciously aid me to turn towards Thee. I was as one dead, Thou didst quicken me with the water of life. I was withered, Thou didst revive me with the heavenly stream of Thine utterance which hath flowed forth from the Pen of the All-Merciful.[29]

His bounty and His justice

The opportunity to know and to love God is a result of His bounty, while the freedom He has given us to choose is the result of His justice. Bahá'í scholar Adib Taherzadeh explains:

> Bahá'u'lláh affirms that God, through His bounty, sends His Manifestations to the world of humanity so that They may reveal His teachings and exhort men to follow the right way. But man in this life has been given freedom of choice. He can choose the path of truth or tarry in the wilderness of self and passion. Whichever path he selects, God will assist him through His justice. For it would be unjust if the Almighty forced His servants to change their ways. This statement throws light on the relationship of the two attributes of God, His bounty and His justice.[30]

Finally, there is the reminder that this is not a relationship between equals; that while *man* needs God, the Creator is above any such limitation. The bounty of God is always present, but whether or not we receive it is entirely up to us.

> ... the bestowals of God are moving and circulating throughout all created things. This illimitable divine bounty has no beginning and will have no ending. It is moving, circulating and becomes effective wherever capacity is developed to receive it.[31]

> Let him that seeketh, attain it; and as to him that hath refused to seek it – verily, God is Self-Sufficient, above any need of His creatures.[32]

If the object of the search is to be attained, man's spiritual senses need to be awakened.

> The fountain of divine generosity is gushing forth, but we must have thirst for the living waters. Unless there be thirst, the salutary water will not assuage. Unless the soul hungers, the delicious foods of the heavenly table will not give sustenance. Unless the eyes of perception be opened, the lights of the sun will not be witnessed. Until the nostrils are purified, the fragrance of the divine rose garden will not be inhaled. Unless the heart be filled with longing, the favours of the Lord will not be evident.[33]

Spiritual awakening – seeing the signs of God

> The spiritually awakened are like to bright torches in the sight of God, they give light and comfort to their fellows.[34]

> This is the fruit of the tree of creation – to be freed from the darkness of the planet in order to enter the worlds of light. This is the object of existence; this is the fruit of the tree of humanity.[35]

It is the 'eye of inner vision', a faculty of the soul, which enables it to become aware of the signs of God around it. If this faculty remains veiled for whatever reason, then the soul will not be awakened, and the search will not begin. It is evident from the condition of society today that many people remain veiled or 'spiritually asleep'; however, if those veils are removed, the transformation of the human reality will begin, through a process of spiritual growth and development.

This transformation of man's character is the whole object of life.

> The rewards of this life are the virtues and perfections which adorn the reality of man. For example, he was dark and becomes luminous; he was ignorant and becomes wise; he was neglectful and becomes vigilant, he was asleep and becomes awakened, he was dead and becomes living; he was blind and becomes a seer; he was deaf and becomes a hearer; he was earthly and becomes heavenly; he was material and becomes spiritual. Through these rewards he gains spiritual birth and becomes a new creature. He becomes the manifestation of the verse in the Gospel where it is said of the disciples that they 'were born, not of blood, nor of the will of the flesh, nor of the will of man, but of God' – that is to say, they were delivered from the animal characteristics and qualities which are the characteristics of human nature, and they became qualified with the divine characteristics, which are the bounty of God. This is the meaning of the second birth.[36]

The spiritual meaning of oppression

Although the prophets appear so that 'spirituality may be infused into the hearts of men',[37] clearly this does not always happen. Some have no interest in God or religion, while the hearts of many are completely occupied with other attachments. Another factor which affects the degree of spiritual susceptibility is the social environment. Bahá'u'lláh referred to this when he described the spiritual climate of society as being a climate of 'oppression'. He quoted the prophetic words of Christ as recorded in the New Testament (Matt.24:29), and outlined the various signs of this condition existing presently in the world.

> As to the words – 'Immediately after the oppression of those days' – they refer to the time when men shall become oppressed and afflicted, the time when the lingering traces of the Sun of Truth and the fruit of the Tree of knowledge and wisdom will have vanished from the midst of men, when the reins of mankind will have fallen into the grasp of the foolish and ignorant, when the portals of divine unity and understanding – the essential and highest purpose in creation – will have been closed, when certain knowledge will have given way to idle fancy, and corruption will have usurped the station of righteousness. Such a condition as this is witnessed in this day when the reins of every community have fallen into the grasp of foolish leaders, who lead after their own whims and desire. On their tongue the mention of God hath become an empty name; in their midst His holy Word a dead letter. Such is the sway of their desires, that the lamp of conscience and reason hath been quenched in their hearts . . .[38]

He links this absence of knowledge and awareness of God in society to the worst form of spiritual oppression.

> What 'oppression' is more grievous than that a soul seeking the truth, and wishing to attain unto the knowledge of God, should know not where to go for it and from whom to seek it?[39]

This condition of oppression existing in the world has come about because humanity has turned away from religion, '. . . the chief instrument for the establishment of order in the world and of tranquillity amongst its peoples,'[40] and therefore has turned away from God. 'Should the lamp of religion be obscured', He writes, 'chaos and confusion will ensue, and the lights of fairness and justice, of tranquillity and peace cease to shine.'[41]

The consequences of putting out the light of religion in men's hearts are reflected in the gross changes in people's behaviour:

> The perversion of human nature, the degradation of human conduct, the corruption and dissolution of human institutions, reveal themselves, under such circumstances, in their worst and most revolting aspects. Human character is debased, confidence is shaken, the nerves of discipline are relaxed, the voice of human conscience is stilled, the sense of decency and shame is obscured, conceptions of duty, of solidarity, of reciprocity and loyalty are distorted, and the very feeling of peacefulness, of joy and of hope is gradually extinguished.[42]

Such conditions increase the climate of oppression, making it so much more difficult for those who are seeking to find the truth, and if the desire in the soul for spiritual truth is not fulfilled, people will seek to satisfy that inner yearning in other ways. In young people that search can lead to substance abuse and in extreme cases individuals will even contemplate suicide when they can find absolutely no meaning to their existence.

Restlessness of the human spirit

If the heart is strongly attached to the material world, then it will not easily be spiritually awakened; it will however remain restless, since it has yet to satisfy the purpose for which it exists, which is to love God. Ultimately, the cause of this restlessness is related to the revelation of the Word of God.

> . . . the Word of God hath infused such awesome power into the inmost essence of humankind that He hath stripped men's human qualities of all effect, and hath, with His all-conquering might, unified the peoples in a vast sea of oneness.[43]

> . . . this spirit of life infusing all created things shall quicken humanity . . .[44]

> The world's equilibrium hath been upset through the vibrating influence of this most great, this new World Order.[45]

In certain passages, the effect of this revelation upon humanity is likened to the effect on living creatures of the heat generated by the sun.

This, however, is but the beginning of the dawn, and the heat of the rising Orb of Truth is not yet at the fullness of its power. Once the sun hath mounted to high noon, its fires will burn so hot as to stir even the creeping things beneath the earth; and although it is not for them to behold the light, yet will they all be set in frenzied motion by the impact of the heat.[46]

This restlessness causes many to search for knowledge and enlightenment, but most people will investigate almost anything, turn in every direction *except* in that direction, towards that horizon which yields true knowledge and spiritual certitude, namely, the ocean of the revealed Word of God.

> People for the most part delight in superstitions. They regard a single drop of the sea of delusion as preferable to an ocean of certitude.[47]

The human spirit will remain in this condition of restlessness until the object of the search is attained.

> O Son of Man! Wert thou to speed through the immensity of space and traverse the expanse of heaven, yet thou wouldst find no rest save in submission to Our command and humbleness before Our Face.[48]

> O Son of Justice! Whither can a lover go but to the land of his beloved? and what seeker findeth rest away from his heart's desire? To the true lover reunion is life, and separation is death. His breast is void of patience and his heart hath no peace. A myriad lives he would forsake to hasten to the abode of his beloved.[49]

Spiritual blindness

There are those, however, who do not even begin the search; they seem to be blind to the existence of the great spiritual forces released into the world through the appearance of the Messengers of God.

> How strange that while the Beloved is visible as the sun, yet the heedless still hunt after tinsel and base metal. Yea, the intensity of His revelation hath covered Him, and the fullness of His shining forth hath hidden Him.

> Even as the sun, bright hath He shined,
> But alas, He hath come to the town of the blind![50]

> The grace of God is beating down upon mankind, even as the rains in spring, and the rays of the manifest Light have made this earth to be the envy of heaven. But alas, the blind are deprived of this bounty, the heedless are closed off from it, the withered despair of it, the faded are dying away – so that even as flooding waters, this endless stream of grace passeth back into its primal source in a hidden sea. Only a few receive this grace and take their share of it.[51]

When man goes through life without any appreciation of his spiritual nature he fails to realize the great power latent within him. An appropriate analogy would be that of travelling through a dark place carrying a powerful torch that has not been switched on.

> I pray that your inner sight may become clear, that you may be able to perceive things the heedless do not see, that you may understand the infinite worlds of God. A man who has no knowledge of the heavenly universe has missed a portion of his heritage and is like unto a stone which knows nothing of humanity.[52]

First birth and second birth

> When a man is born into the world of phenomena he finds the universe; when he is born from this world to the world of the spirit, he finds the Kingdom.[53]

New worlds are revealed to the soul that is awakened and begins to develop spiritual capacities. The sooner these spiritual faculties are used, the sooner man will become aware of the existence of that higher world and achieve the happiness he seeks.

> If he attains rebirth while in the world of nature, he will become informed of the divine world. He will observe that another and a higher world exists. Wonderful bounties descend; eternal life awaits; everlasting glory surrounds him. All the signs of reality and greatness are there. He will see the lights of God. All these experiences will be

his when he is born out of the world of nature into the divine world. Therefore, for the perfect man there are two kinds of birth: the first, physical birth, is from the matrix of the mother; the second, or spiritual birth, is from the world of nature. In both he is without knowledge of the new world of existence he is entering. Therefore, rebirth means his release from the captivity of nature, freedom from attachment to this mortal and material life. This is the second, or spiritual, birth of which Jesus Christ spoke in the Gospels.[54]

For the essential reality is the spirit, the foundation is the spirit, the life of man is due to the spirit; the happiness, the animus, the radiance, the glory of man – all are due to the spirit; and if in the spirit no reformation takes place, there will be no result to human existence.[55]

CHAPTER 6

THE EFFECT OF VEILS

> The spiritual world is like unto the phenomenal world. They are the exact counterpart of each other. Whatever objects appear in this world of existence are the outer pictures of the world of heaven.[1]

> The outer sun is a sign or symbol of the inner and ideal Sun of Truth, the Word of God.[2]

In the physical world, veils act as barriers, hiding and obscuring from sight the things over which they fall. Spiritually, veils operate in much the same way; they cover and obscure the soul from the light of God. The relationship between the soul and the power which illumines it is summed up in the Writings by the recurring analogy of the mirror and the sun.

> Souls are like unto mirrors, and the bounty of God is like unto the sun.[3]

Just as a plant needs sunshine to grow, if the soul is to grow and develop it must receive the light of God. Man's ability to discover those attributes hidden in the soul depends on two things: first, the Messenger of God must appear and shine the light of divine guidance.

> The holy Manifestations of God come into the world to dispel the darkness of the animal, or physical, nature of man, to purify him from his imperfections in order that his heavenly and spiritual nature may become quickened, his divine qualities awakened, his perfections visible, his potential powers revealed and all the virtues of the world of humanity latent within him may come to life.[4]

Secondly, man must turn the mirror of his soul towards that light.

> . . . if you turn the mirror of your spirits heavenwards, the heavenly constellations and the rays of the Sun of Reality will be reflected in your hearts, and the virtues of the Kingdom will be obtained.[5]

If the soul is veiled, then the light of divine guidance will *not* shine in it and man's spiritual potential will not be awakened.

> The bestowals of God are all and always manifest. The promises of heaven are ever present. The favours of God are all-surrounding, but should the conscious eye of the soul of man remain veiled and darkened, he will be led to deny these universal signs and remain deprived of these manifestations of divine bounty. Therefore, we must endeavour with heart and soul in order that the veil covering the eye of inner vision may be removed, that we may behold the manifestations of the signs of God, discern His mysterious graces and realize that material blessings as compared with spiritual bounties are as nothing. The spiritual blessings of God are greatest.[6]

The fact is that it is unnatural for man not to seek after spiritual knowledge, because he was created for that purpose. To deny that truth, to live life in an entirely material way without acknowledging either God or the existence of the soul goes against part of man's intrinsic nature; it is a denial of his true spiritual reality. Man is a spiritual being and is destined eventually to exist in a spiritual environment, which is why living in this world is such a challenge for him; yet God has intended that he complete this physical journey and if man is to realize his true potential in this life, then he must come to understand the effect that veils have on his spiritual reality.

The potential of the soul

The physical growth and development of the human embryo provides some insight into the mystery of the development of the soul. The human embryo has an amazing potential; it begins as a single cell, yet it grows into a complex body with many physical attributes. Likewise the soul, although undeveloped to begin with, has a tremendous potential to grow, develop, and manifest powers and qualities. The growth of the seed is another example used in the Writings to illustrate this principle of the hidden potential of the soul.

The virtues of the seed are revealed in the tree; it puts forth branches, leaves, blossoms, and produces fruits. All these virtues were hidden and potential in the seed. Through the blessing and bounty of cultivation these virtues became apparent. Similarly, the merciful God, our Creator, has deposited within human realities certain latent and potential virtues. Through education and culture these virtues deposited by the loving God will become apparent in the human reality, even as the unfoldment of the tree from within the germinating seed.[7]

Man has two powers; and his development, two aspects. One power is connected with the material world, and by it he is capable of material advancement. The other power is spiritual, and through its development his inner, potential nature is awakened. These powers are like two wings. Both must be developed, for flight is impossible with one wing.[8]

The obscuring dust

The most important thing is to polish the mirrors of hearts in order that they may become illumined and receptive of the divine light. One heart may possess the capacity of the polished mirror; another, be covered and obscured by the dust and dross of this world.[9]

Those things which prevent the light of the Sun of Truth from illuminating the soul are likened in the Writings to the dust and dross that accumulate on the surface of a mirror. In spiritual terms that dust is man's attachment to this world, an attachment which gradually erodes his spiritual susceptibilities.

What is the dust which obscures the mirror? It is attachment to the world, avarice, envy, love of luxury and comfort, haughtiness and self-desire; this is the dust which prevents reflection of the rays of the Sun of Reality in the mirror. The natural emotions are blameworthy and are like rust which deprives the heart of the bounties of God. But sincerity, justice, humility, severance, and love for the believers of God will purify the mirror and make it radiant with reflected rays from the Sun of Truth.[10]

... the more he becomes immersed in material progress, the more does his spirituality become obscured.[11]

The barriers between God and man

Commenting on the barriers which come between man and God, Adib Taherzadeh writes:

> The possession of earthly goods is often misunderstood to be the only form of attachment. But this is not so. Man's pride in his accomplishments, his knowledge, his position, his popularity within society and, above all, his love for his own self are some of the barriers which come between him and God. To rid oneself of these attachments is not easy. It can be a painful process and may indeed prove to be a spiritual battle which lasts a lifetime.
>
> Whereas riches may become a mighty barrier between man and God, and rich people are often in great danger of attachment, yet people with small worldly possessions can also become attached to material things. The following Persian story of a king and a dervish[*] illustrates this. Once there was a king who had many spiritual qualities and whose deeds were based on justice and loving-kindness. He often envied the dervish who had renounced the world and appeared to be free from the cares of this material life, for he roamed the country, slept in any place when night fell and chanted the praises of his Lord during the day. He lived in poverty, yet thought he owned the whole world. His only possessions were his clothes and a basket in which he carried the food donated by his well-wishers. The king was attracted to this way of life.
>
> Once he invited a well-known dervish to his palace, sat at his feet and begged him for some lessons about detachment. The dervish was delighted with the invitation. He stayed a few days in the palace and whenever the king was free preached the virtues of a mendicant's life to him. At last the king was converted. One day, dressed in the garb of a poor man, he left his palace in the company of the dervish. They had walked together some distance when the dervish realized that he had

---

[*] A mystic who renounces the world in order to commune with God, subsisting on the charity of his fellow men.

left his basket behind in the palace. This disturbed him greatly and, informing the king that he could not go without his basket, he begged permission to return for it. But the king admonished him, saying that he himself had left behind his palaces, his wealth and power, whereas the dervish, who had preached for a lifetime the virtues of detachment, had at last been tested and was found to be attached to this world – his small basket.[12]

The veil of material wealth

Material prosperity, especially when earned through one's livelihood, is the natural right of every human being and it is not expected that people should reject the benefits of material civilization in order to become spiritual. However, the lower nature of man is strongly attracted to the material world and the desire to acquire can become so all-consuming that it may turn the soul away from God.

Some people equate happiness with acquiring material wealth, when in reality that goal can become a trap. To think that possessing a certain thing or attaining to a particular level of wealth will bring happiness is a delusion, because acquisition does not satisfy. That is the consequence of making one's happiness dependent upon material wealth; however much is gained, it is never enough – it *can* never be enough. Things which are merely material compositions cannot ever satisfy the deep need of the soul for spiritual sustenance.

> Verily I say, the world is like the vapour in a desert, which the thirsty dreameth to be water and striveth after it with all his might, until when he cometh unto it, he findeth it to be mere illusion. It may, moreover, be likened unto the lifeless image of the beloved whom the lover hath sought and found, in the end, after long search and to his utmost regret, to be such as cannot 'fatten nor appease his hunger'.[13]

> O Friends! Abandon not the everlasting beauty for a beauty that must die, and set not your affections on this mortal world of dust.[14]

There are other barriers or veils besides material things which can come between man and God. Some examples of these veils are:

- the veil of knowledge

- the veil of self

- the veil of language.

The veil of knowledge

In one of His books Bahá'u'lláh described 'knowledge' as: 'this densest of all veils . . . the veil referred to in the saying: "The most grievous of all veils is the veil of knowledge."'[15]

When man turns the powers of the mind towards the acquisition of knowledge which excludes the knowledge of God, that acquired knowledge can become a barrier between the soul and God.

> How vast the number of the learned who have turned aside from the way of God and how numerous the men devoid of learning who have apprehended the truth . . .[16]

In the Writings, the truly learned are identified as those who do not let their knowledge and learning prevent them from believing in God.

> Blessed is the wayfarer who hath recognized the Desired One, and the seeker who hath heeded the Call of Him Who is the intended Aim of all mankind, and the learned one who hath believed in God, the Help in Peril, the Self-Subsisting.[17]

> Although to acquire the sciences and arts is the greatest glory of mankind, this is so only on condition that man's river flow into the mighty sea, and draw from God's ancient source His inspiration. When this cometh to pass, then every teacher is as a shoreless ocean, every pupil a prodigal fountain of knowledge. If, then, the pursuit of knowledge lead to the beauty of Him Who is the Object of all Knowledge, how excellent that goal; but if not, a mere drop will perhaps shut a man off from flooding grace, for with learning cometh arrogance and pride, and it bringeth on error and indifference to God.
>
> The sciences of today are bridges to reality; if then they lead not to reality, naught remains but fruitless illusion. By the one true God!

> If learning be not a means of access to Him, the Most Manifest, it is nothing but evident loss.[18]

The arrogance or pride that can accompany the acquisition of knowledge feeds the ego, and the attachment of people to their own cleverness may in the end become a dense veil causing them to deny God, and thus shutting themselves off from His bounty.

> The most burning fire is to question the signs of God, to dispute idly that which He hath revealed, to deny Him and carry one's self proudly before Him.[19]

The veil of self

Commenting on the subject of 'self-love', 'Abdu'l-Bahá stated:

> This is a strange trait and the means of the destruction of many important souls in the world. If man be imbued with all good qualities but be selfish, all the other virtues will fade or pass away and eventually he will grow worse.[20]

In the following excerpt, 'Abdu'l-Bahá says that 'egotism' is like rust, but that the tests of life can remove that rust from the hearts of the sincere.

> . . . trials are as the gift of God, the Exalted; but for weak souls they are an unexpected calamity. This test is just as thou hast written: it removeth the rust of egotism from the mirror of the heart until the Sun of Truth may shine therein. For, no veil is greater than egotism and no matter how thin that covering may be, yet it will finally veil man entirely and prevent him from receiving a portion from the eternal bounty.[21]

Another passage from the Writings states:

> . . . the complete and entire elimination of the ego would imply perfection – which man can never completely attain – but the ego can and should be ever-increasingly subordinated to the enlightened soul of man. This is what spiritual progress implies.[22]

The veil of language

> One of the veils is literal interpretation.[23]

While the veil of knowledge and the veil of self are created by man's choices, the veil of language is associated with the revelation of the Word of God and is one of the means by which God tests the purity of the hearts of men.

> Know verily that the purpose underlying all these symbolic terms and abstruse allusions, which emanate from the Revealers of God's holy Cause, hath been to test and prove the peoples of the world; that thereby the earth of the pure and illuminated hearts may be known from the perishable and barren soil. From time immemorial such hath been the way of God amidst His creatures, and to this testify the records of the sacred books.[24]

The Word of God is a mysterious power; it can bring great happiness through the knowledge it bestows. However, it can also be very challenging, since the words have spiritual meanings, which may not be immediately apparent. Bahá'u'lláh revealed that the language of the Messengers of God is twofold:

> One language, the outward language, is devoid of allusions, is unconcealed and unveiled; that it may be a guiding lamp and a beaconing light . . . The other language is veiled and concealed . . . This is the divine standard, this is the Touchstone of God, wherewith He proveth His servants. None apprehendeth the meaning of these utterances except them whose hearts are assured, whose souls have found favour with God, and whose minds are detached from all else but Him. In such utterances, the literal meaning, as generally understood by the people, is not what hath been intended.[25]

Reading the words without understanding them can eventually lead to doctrines being formed which bear no relationship to the intended meaning, for instance, the belief in a physical resurrection of bodies which is preached in many churches. If the words 'life' and 'death' were to be taken literally, how could, for example, Christ's statement 'let the dead bury their dead'[26] be understood?

Clearly, many passages in the Holy Books have meanings other than the literal:

> The divine Words are not to be taken according to their outer sense. They are symbolical and contain realities of spiritual meaning. For instance, in the book of Solomon's songs you will read about the bride and bridegroom. It is evident that the physical bride and bridegroom are not intended. Obviously, these are symbols conveying a hidden and inner significance. In the same way the Revelations of St. John are not to be taken literally, but spiritually. These are the mysteries of God.[27]

Another example of a failure to understand the spiritual meaning of the texts (which had profound consequences) can be seen in the interpretation by the Jews of the Old Testament prophecies regarding the appearance of Christ.

> Be not satisfied with words, but seek to understand the spiritual meanings hidden in the heart of the words. The Jews read the Old Testament night and day, memorizing its words and texts yet without comprehending a single meaning or inner significance, for had they understood the real meanings of the Old Testament, they would have become believers in Christ, inasmuch as the Old Testament was revealed to prepare His coming . . .[28]

Language can be a significant veil, but it must be remembered that understanding the Word of God is not dependent upon having a superior education; the essential requirement is to have a pure heart.

> The understanding of His words and the comprehension of the utterances of the Birds of Heaven are in no wise dependent upon human learning. They depend solely upon purity of heart, chastity of soul, and freedom of spirit.[29]

Distracted and diverted

All these veils tend to divert and distract man from the true objective of his life. He becomes careless of matters concerning his soul. During His visit to New York 'Abdu'l-Bahá admonished the peoples of the world on account of this carelessness:

> Is it not astonishing that although man has been created for the knowledge and love of God, for the virtues of the human world, for spirituality, heavenly illumination and eternal life, nevertheless, he continues ignorant and negligent of all this? Consider how he seeks knowledge of everything except knowledge of God. For instance, his utmost desire is to penetrate the mysteries of the lowest strata of the earth . . . He puts forth arduous labours to fathom terrestrial mysteries but is not at all concerned about knowing the mysteries of the Kingdom, traversing the illimitable fields of the eternal world, becoming informed of the divine realities, discovering the secrets of God, attaining the knowledge of God, witnessing the splendours of the Sun of Truth and realizing the glories of everlasting life. He is unmindful and thoughtless of these. How much he is attracted to the mysteries of matter and how completely unaware he is of the mysteries of divinity! . . . It is as if a kind and loving father had provided a library of wonderful books for his son in order that he might be informed of the mysteries of creation; at the same time surrounding him with every means of comfort and enjoyment; but the son amuses himself with pebbles and playthings, neglectful of all his father's gifts and provision. How ignorant and heedless is man! The Father has willed for him eternal glory, and he is content with blindness and deprivation. The Father has built for him a royal palace, but he is playing with the dust; prepared for him garments of silk, but he prefers to remain unclothed; provided for him delicious foods and fruits, while he seeks sustenance in the grasses of the field.[30]

Spiritual blindness and neglect of the true self (the higher nature) will in the end prove to be the greatest deprivation of all.

> And be ye not like those who forget God, and whom He hath therefore caused to forget their own selves.[31]

To become forgetful of our true selves is to deprive ourselves of our spiritual heritage. In order to appreciate the significance of this, the next chapter will examine various passages from the Writings on the subject of soul, mind and spirit.

CHAPTER 7

SOUL, MIND AND SPIRIT

All things below the human kingdom are subject to the laws of nature; they cannot escape those forces, nor can they understand them. Man is different. The essential difference between the human kingdom and the animal kingdom is the human rational soul which empowers man to do what no animal could possibly do. It is the discovering power of the soul which distinguishes man from all other forms of phenomenal life, as the following quotations illustrate.

> The animal can only know through sense impressions and cannot grasp intellectual realities. The animal cannot conceive of the power of thought. This is an abstract intellectual matter and not limited to the senses. The animal is incapable of knowing that the earth is round. In brief, abstract intellectual phenomena are human powers. All creation below the kingdom of man is the captive of nature; it cannot deviate in the slightest degree from nature's laws. But man wrests the sword of dominion from nature's hand and uses it upon nature's head. For example, it is a natural exigency that man should be a dweller upon the earth, but the power of the human spirit transcends this limitation, and he soars aloft in airplanes. This is contrary to the law and requirement of nature. He sails at high speed upon the ocean and dives beneath its surface in submarines. He imprisons the human voice in a phonograph and communicates in the twinkling of an eye from East to West. These are things we know to be contrary to the limitations of natural law. Man transcends nature, while the mineral, vegetable and animal are helplessly subject to it. This can be done only through the power of the spirit, because the spirit is the reality.[1]

> For all created things except man are subjects or captives of nature; they

cannot deviate in the slightest degree from nature's law and control. The colossal sun, centre of our planetary system, is nature's captive, incapable of the least variation from the law of command. All the orbs and luminaries in this illimitable universe are, likewise, obedient to nature's regulation.[2]

For instance, the animal cannot conceive of the earth whereon it stands as a spherical object because the spherical shape of the earth is a matter of conscious reasoning. It is not a matter of sense perception. An animal in Europe could not foresee and plan the discovery of America as Columbus did . . . The animal cannot become aware of the fact that the earth is revolving and the sun stationary. Only processes of reasoning can come to this conclusion. The outward eye sees the sun as revolving. It mistakes the stars and the planets as moving about the earth. But reason decides their orbit, knows that the earth is moving and the other worlds fixed, knows that the sun is the solar centre and ever occupies the same place, proves that it is the earth which revolves around it. Such conclusions are entirely intellectual, not according to the senses.[3]

As the soul is a sign of God, we are unable to comprehend it

The soul is an enduring mystery; much as we might wish to comprehend it, Bahá'u'lláh defines our limitations in this regard in quite emphatic language:

> Wert thou to ponder in thine heart, from now until the end that hath no end, and with all the concentrated intelligence and understanding which the greatest minds have attained in the past or will attain in the future, this divinely ordained and subtle Reality, this sign of the revelation of the All-Abiding, All-Glorious God, thou wilt fail to comprehend its mystery or to appraise its virtue.[4]

Having read this statement, it has to be accepted that the true nature of the soul is completely hidden from us; yet, what *has* been written about it in the Writings enables us to understand to a limited degree some of its qualities and attributes.

The three terms *soul*, *mind* and *spirit* are used throughout the Writings to describe different aspects of the human reality. Additionally, the terms *rational soul*, *human spirit* and even *human rational soul* are also used.

The distinguishing power

> The human spirit which distinguishes man from the animal is the rational soul; and these two names – the human spirit and the rational soul – designate one thing. This spirit, which in the terminology of the philosophers is the rational soul, embraces all beings, and as far as human ability permits discovers the realities of things and becomes cognizant of their peculiarities and effects, and of the qualities and properties of beings. But the human spirit, unless assisted by the spirit of faith, does not become acquainted with the divine secrets and the heavenly realities. It is like a mirror which, although clear, polished, and brilliant, is still in need of light. Until a ray of the sun reflects upon it, it cannot discover the heavenly secrets.[5]

In order to appreciate what is meant by the term 'human spirit', we can look at other references in which 'Abdu'l-Bahá differentiates between forms of spirit.[6] He explains that spirit manifests itself in varying degrees throughout the different kingdoms. For example, in the mineral kingdom that spirit is cohesion, in the vegetable kingdom it is the power of growth and in the animal kingdom, not only growth but also the outer senses of sight, hearing, smell, taste and touch.

This evolution in complexity and power from the lowest kingdom upwards reflects '. . . the law of progress; how all moves from the inferior to the superior degree',[7] and 'progress', 'Abdu'l-Bahá explained, 'is the expression of spirit in the world of matter'.[8]

In summary, the expression of spirit in the human kingdom is far superior to that in the animal kingdom due to the distinguishing faculty of the rational soul, and this truth is confirmed and restated in many passages throughout the Writings.

The power of life

> The spirit is the power of life.[9]

Man is described as having both a human spirit and an animal spirit – 'animal spirit' meaning the spirit which is responsible for the growth and development of man's physical body, just as in animals.

> The human spirit may be likened to the bounty of the sun shining on a mirror. The body of man, which is composed from the elements, is combined and mingled in the most perfect form; it is the most solid construction, the noblest combination, the most perfect existence. It grows and develops through the animal spirit. This perfected body can be compared to a mirror, and the human spirit to the sun.[10]

When the physical body of a human being dies and begins to decompose, it is that 'animal' aspect of spirit which ceases, just as it does when an animal dies:

> After the dissociation and decomposition of the combined elements this spirit also will naturally disappear. It is like this lamp which you see: when the oil and wick and fire are brought together, light is the result; but when the oil is finished and the wick consumed, the light will also vanish and be lost.[11]

The human spirit (the soul), however, carries on after the death of the body.

The power to acquire

> But the spirit of man has two aspects: one divine, one satanic – that is to say, it is capable of the utmost perfection, or it is capable of the utmost imperfection. If it acquires virtues, it is the most noble of the existing beings; and if it acquires vices, it becomes the most degraded existence.[12]

The two natures in man are described as the 'personal ego' and the 'divine ego'.

> As long as man is a captive of habit, pursuing the dictates of self and desire, he is vanquished and defeated. This passionate personal ego takes the reins from his hands, crowds out the qualities of the divine ego and changes him into an animal, a creature unable to judge good from evil, or to distinguish light from darkness. He becomes blind to divine attributes, for this acquired individuality, the result of an evil routine of thought, becomes the dominant note of his life.[13]

This explanation sums up the great struggle in life and reveals the tension that exists between these two natures in man.¹⁴ From one nature comes the spiritual qualities, and from the other, the material qualities.

Exercise strengthens, while neglect results in weakening

When the spiritual qualities are used they become stronger, while the material qualities become weaker. The converse is also true.

> . . . if the spiritual qualities of the soul, open to the breath of the Divine Spirit, are never used, they become atrophied, enfeebled, and at last incapable; whilst the soul's material qualities alone being exercised, they become terribly powerful – and the unhappy, misguided man, becomes more savage, more unjust, more vile, more cruel, more malevolent than the lower animals themselves. All his aspirations and desires being strengthened by the lower side of the soul's nature, he becomes more and more brutal, until his whole being is in no way superior to that of the beasts that perish. Men such as this, plan to work evil, to hurt and to destroy; they are entirely without the spirit of Divine compassion, for the celestial quality of the soul has been dominated by that of the material. If, on the contrary, the spiritual nature of the soul has been so strengthened that it holds the material side in subjection, then does the man approach the Divine; his humanity becomes so glorified that the virtues of the Celestial Assembly are manifested in him; he radiates the Mercy of God, he stimulates the spiritual progress of mankind, for he becomes a lamp to show light on their path.¹⁵

The intellectual power of the rational soul

It is evident that the soul has many facets, and the different terms used in the Writings to describe it reflect the variety of its powers and functions. For example, in this next quotation, 'Abdu'l-Bahá comments on another power of the 'rational soul', demonstrating that:

- it is an 'intellectual' and 'discovering' power

- it is a power which manifests itself in this world through the human reality

- it is 'the greatest power of perception in the world of nature', and

- every human being without exception possesses this intellectual power.

The first condition of perception in the world of nature is the perception of the rational soul. In this perception and in this power all men are sharers, whether they be neglectful or vigilant, believers or deniers. This human rational soul is God's creation; it encompasses and excels other creatures; as it is more noble and distinguished, it encompasses things. The power of the rational soul can discover the realities of things, comprehend the peculiarities of beings, and penetrate the mysteries of existence. All sciences, knowledge, arts, wonders, institutions, discoveries and enterprises come from the exercised intelligence of the rational soul. There was a time when they were unknown, preserved mysteries and hidden secrets; the rational soul gradually discovered them and brought them out from the plane of the invisible and the hidden into the realm of the visible. This is the greatest power of perception in the world of nature, which in its highest flight and soaring comprehends the realities, the properties and the effects of the contingent beings.[16]

The rational soul is the 'intermediary' between the body and the spirit

'Abdu'l-Bahá also confirms that the 'human intelligence' and the 'rational soul' are the same thing, and explains that it functions as the intermediary between the physical body and the spirit.

> There are in the world of humanity three degrees; those of the body, the soul, and spirit.
>
> The body is the physical or animal degree of man . . . Like the animal, man possesses the faculties of the senses, is subject to heat, cold, hunger, thirst, etc.; unlike the animal, man has a rational soul, the human intelligence.
>
> This intelligence of man is the intermediary between his body and his spirit.
>
> When man allows the spirit, through his soul, to enlighten his understanding, then does he contain all Creation . . .[17]

SOUL, MIND AND SPIRIT

You perceive how the soul is the intermediary between the body and the spirit. In like manner is this tree the intermediary between the seed and the fruit . . . When a soul has in it the life of the spirit, then does it bring forth good fruit and become a Divine tree.[18]

While in some passages in the Writings 'soul' and 'spirit' seem to have been used in such a way as to suggest they are one and the same thing, we note that in this talk 'Abdu'l-Bahá distinguished between them.[19]

How does the soul function as an intermediary?

First, 'Abdu'l-Bahá addresses the relationship between the outer physical powers and the inner spiritual powers:

> In man five outer powers exist, which are the agents of perception — that is to say, through these five powers man perceives material beings. These are sight, which perceives visible forms; hearing, which perceives audible sounds; smell, which perceives odours; taste, which perceives foods; and feeling, which is in all parts of the body and perceives tangible things. These five powers perceive outward existences.[20]

Next, five powers of the *soul* are identified: *imagination, thought, comprehension, memory* and the *common faculty*, the specific spiritual power which acts as the intermediary agent being the *common faculty*.

> Man has also spiritual powers: imagination, which conceives things; thought, which reflects upon realities; comprehension, which comprehends realities; memory, which retains whatever man imagines, thinks, and comprehends. The intermediary between the five outward powers and the inward powers is the sense which they possess in common — that is to say, the sense which acts between the outer and inner powers, conveys to the inward powers whatever the outer powers discern. It is termed the common faculty, because it communicates between the outward and inward powers and thus is common to the outward and inward powers.[21]

On another occasion, speaking on the subject of healing, 'Abdu'l-Bahá indicated that the sympathetic nervous system was a *common system* in that it was susceptible to both physical and spiritual influence:

> The powers of the sympathetic nerve are neither entirely physical nor spiritual, but are between the two (systems). The nerve is connected with both. Its phenomena shall be perfect when its spiritual and physical relations are normal.
>
> When the material world and the divine world are well co-related, when the hearts become heavenly and the aspirations grow pure and divine, perfect connection shall take place. Then shall this power produce a perfect manifestation. Physical and spiritual diseases will then receive absolute healing.[22]

The soul has two means of perception

The soul can operate in two modes; it can work either through the physical body with the aid of the common faculty (what 'Abdu'l-Bahá calls *instrumentality*), or entirely without involving the physical body – *independently*.

> Furthermore, this immortal human soul is endowed with two means of perception: One is effected through instrumentality; the other, independently. For instance, the soul sees through the instrumentality of the eye, hears with the ear, smells through the nostrils and grasps objects with the hands. These are the actions or operations of the soul through instruments. But in the world of dreams the soul sees when the eyes are closed. The man is seemingly dead, lies there as dead; the ears do not hear, yet he hears. The body lies there, but he – that is, the soul – travels, sees, observes. All the instruments of the body are inactive, all the functions seemingly useless. Notwithstanding this, there is an immediate and vivid perception by the soul. Exhilaration is experienced. The soul journeys, perceives, senses. It often happens that a man in a state of wakefulness has not been able to accomplish the solution of a problem, and when he goes to sleep, he will reach that solution in a dream. How often it has happened that he has dreamed, even as the prophets have dreamed, of the future; and events which have thus been foreshadowed have come to pass literally.[23]

The power to operate independently of the body

As the above quotation reveals, even without the body, the soul can *perceive*, *sense*, *move* and *discover*.

In the *Seven Valleys*, a particularly mystical composition from the pen of Bahá'u'lláh which traces man's spiritual journey of discovery, we find another reference to the power of the soul to operate independently of the body:

> O friend, wert thou to taste of these fruits . . . which grow in the lands of knowledge, . . . yearning would seize the reins of patience and reserve from out thy hand, and make thy soul to shake with the flashing light, and draw thee from the earthly homeland to the first, heavenly abode in the Centre of Realities, and lift thee to a plane wherein thou wouldst soar in the air even as thou walkest upon the earth, and move over the water as thou runnest on the land.[24]

The rider and the steed

Here again, as in the previous passage, the soul is defined by 'Abdu'l-Bahá as an independent power:

> Therefore, we learn that the immortality of the soul, or spirit, is not contingent or dependent upon the so-called immortality of the body, because the body in the quiescent state, in the time of sleep, may be as dead, unconscious, senseless; but the soul, or spirit, is possessed of perceptions, sensations, motion and discovery. Even inspiration and revelation are obtained by it. How many were the prophets who have had marvellous visions of the future while in that state! The spirit, or human soul, is the rider; and the body is only the steed. If anything affects the steed, the rider is not affected by it. The spirit may be likened to the light within the lantern. The body is simply the outer lantern. If the lantern should break, the light is ever the same because the light could shine even without the lantern. The spirit can conduct its affairs without the body. In the world of dreams it is precisely as this light without the chimney glass. It can shine without the glass. The human soul by means of this body can perform its operations, and without the body it can, likewise, have its control. Therefore, if the body be

subject to disintegration, the spirit is not affected by these changes or transformations.[25]

In *this* world, when a person is awake and active the spirit expresses itself through the body and the mind; however, when sleep comes the spirit begins to operate independently of the body.

Activity of the soul and the world of dreams

The activity of the soul during sleep is a great mystery. The following quotations describe how the soul gains access to a spiritual realm hidden within this world while the body is asleep. The nature of that 'realm' remains a mystery, but our lack of understanding of it does not take away from its reality.

> One of the created phenomena is the dream. Behold how many secrets are deposited therein, how many wisdoms treasured up, how many worlds concealed. Observe, how thou art asleep in a dwelling, and its doors are barred; on a sudden thou findest thyself in a far-off city, which thou enterest without moving thy feet or wearying thy body; without using thine eyes, thou seest; without taxing thine ears, thou hearest; without a tongue, thou speakest. And perchance when ten years are gone, thou wilt witness in the outer world the very things thou hast dreamed tonight.[26]

> Consider thy state when asleep. Verily, I say, this phenomenon is the most mysterious of the signs of God amongst men, were they to ponder it in their hearts . . . that thy spirit, having transcended the limitations of sleep and having stripped itself of all earthly attachment, hath, by the act of God, been made to traverse a realm which lieth hidden in the innermost reality of this world. Verily I say, the creation of God embraceth worlds besides this world, and creatures apart from these creatures.[27]

> . . . consider the world of dreams, wherein the body of man is immovable, seemingly dead, not subject to sensation; the eyes do not see, the ears do not hear nor the tongue speak. But the spirit of man is not asleep; it sees, hears, moves, perceives and discovers realities. Therefore, it is evident that the spirit of man is not affected by the change or

condition of the body. Even though the material body should die, the spirit continues eternally alive, just as it exists and functions in the inert body in the realm of dreams. That is to say, the spirit is immortal and will continue its existence after the destruction of the body.[28]

Finally, in the *Seven Valleys*, this statement from the pen of Bahá'u'lláh can be found:

> Likewise, reflect upon the perfection of man's creation, and that all these planes and states are folded up and hidden away within him. 'Dost thou reckon thyself only a puny form when within thee the universe is folded?'[29]

This is the mystery of the soul.

Different avenues of knowledge

The Writings explain that in this world things can be comprehended by the *senses*, by *reason*, by *tradition* (interpreting the written texts) and through *inspiration*.[30]

> . . . in the human material world of phenomena these four are the only existing criteria or avenues of knowledge, and all of them are faulty and unreliable.[31]

Being open to the influence of the Holy Spirit is the only way to attain 'perfect knowledge'.

> What then remains? How shall we attain the reality of knowledge? By the breaths and promptings of the Holy Spirit, which is light and knowledge itself. Through it the human mind is quickened and fortified into true conclusions and perfect knowledge.[32]

In the physical world, the power of sight is only possible when the eyes have access to light. Similarly, all of the divine perfections which God caused to be reflected in the human soul are latent qualities; they will be awakened and revealed *only* when the soul is illumined by the spiritual light which emanates from the kingdom of God.

> Until a ray of the sun reflects upon it, it cannot discover the heavenly secrets.[33]

When that happens, spiritual truths will be understood through that faculty of the soul which 'Abdu'l-Bahá refers to as the 'heavenly intellectual power'.

The natural intellectual power and the heavenly intellectual power

In this passage, 'Abdu'l-Bahá explains that man's intellectual power discovers realities through investigation and research, whereas the heavenly intellectual power is awakened when the soul comes into contact with the Manifestation of God.

> But the universal divine mind, which is beyond nature, is the bounty of the Pre-existent Power. This universal mind is divine; it embraces existing realities, and it receives the light of the mysteries of God. It is a conscious power, not a power of investigation and of research. The intellectual power of the world of nature is a power of investigation, and by its researches it discovers the realities of beings and the properties of existences; but the heavenly intellectual power, which is beyond nature, embraces things and is cognizant of things, knows them, understands them, is aware of mysteries, realities and divine significations, and is the discoverer of the concealed verities of the Kingdom. This divine intellectual power is the special attribute of the Holy Manifestations and the Dawning-places of prophethood; a ray of this light falls upon the mirrors of the hearts of the righteous, and a portion and a share of this power comes to them through the Holy Manifestations.[34]

When the spiritual seeker connects with the Messenger of God the spirit of faith is born in the heart; that soul consciously 'knows' through the 'heavenly intellectual power' that it has come into contact with the divine reality. Faith in God then, is a matter of conscious knowledge.

> Herein lies the difference: By faith is meant, first, conscious knowledge, and second, the practice of good deeds.[35]

If man wishes to soar into the heaven of spiritual knowledge, he must go beyond the limitations of material knowledge and learning, and open his heart to the Word of God. Bahá'u'lláh tells us:

> Weigh not the Book of God with such standards and sciences as are current amongst you, for the Book itself is the unerring balance established amongst men.[36]

> ... man can never hope to attain unto the knowledge of the All-Glorious, can never quaff from the stream of divine knowledge and wisdom, can never enter the abode of immortality, nor partake of the cup of divine nearness and favour, unless and until he ceases to regard the words and deeds of mortal men as a standard for the true understanding and recognition of God and His Prophets.[37]

Contact with the Word of God awakens those qualities lying dormant in the soul, referred to by 'Abdu'l-Bahá as 'the inner susceptibilities'.[38]

> The essential ordinances rest upon the firm, unchanging, eternal foundations of the Word itself. They concern spiritualities, seek to stabilize morals, awaken intuitive susceptibilities, reveal the knowledge of God and inculcate the love of all mankind.[39]

Differences in intellectual capacity

In the human kingdom, people are separated from one another by sex, education, wealth, skin colour, race and many other factors; yet from the spiritual perspective such distinctions are unimportant.

> In reality, God has created all mankind, and in the estimation of God there is no distinction as to male and female.[40]

> He has created all. Assuredly He must have loved them equally; otherwise, He would not have created them.[41]

> ... an equal standard of human rights must be recognized and adopted. In the estimation of God all men are equal; there is no distinction or preferment for any soul in the dominion of His justice and equity.[42]

While on the one hand God bestows his bounty equally upon all, on the other hand he has fashioned every soul to be unique and that individuality is reflected in the differences in capacity.

> It is evident, therefore, that mankind differs in natal capacity and intrinsic intellectual endowment. Nevertheless, although capacities are not the same, every member of the human race is capable of education.[43]

Differences in spiritual capacity

Just as there are differences in intellectual capacity between people, so also there are differences spiritually. Some have a greater capacity than others; however, for everyone the real merit lies in filling the cup they have been given, whatever its size.

> The whole duty of man in this Day is to attain that share of the flood of grace which God poureth forth for him. Let none, therefore, consider the largeness or smallness of the receptacle. The portion of some might lie in the palm of a man's hand, the portion of others might fill a cup, and of others even a gallon-measure.[44]

The soul, being an emanation from the worlds of God, has the capacity to reflect the light of all the names and attributes of God, but the *degree* to which each of those attributes can be reflected will vary from person to person.

> When the infinite effulgences of God are revealed in the individuality of man, then divine attributes, invisible in the rest of creation, become manifest through him and one man becomes the manifestor of knowledge, that is, divine knowledge is revealed to him; another is the dawning place of power; a third is trustworthy; again, one is faithful, and another is merciful. All these attributes are the characteristics of the unchangeable individuality and are divine in origin.[45]

There will even be variations in spiritual progress.

> . . . the differences which exist between men in regard to spiritual progress and heavenly perfections are also due to the choice of the Compassionate One.[46]

This is what distinguishes every human being; it is this combination of unique intellectual capacity and unique spiritual capacity. Each of the divine attributes is revealed to a different degree of intensity in each soul, and those differences result in *individuality*. 'Personality' on the other hand is not a lasting thing as it does not arise from God's attributes.

> The individuality of each created thing is based upon divine wisdom, for in the creation of God there is no defect. However, personality has no element of permanence. It is a slightly changeable quality in man which can be turned in either direction. For if he acquire praiseworthy virtues, these strengthen the individuality of man and call forth his hidden forces; but if he acquire defects, the beauty and simplicity of the individuality will be lost to him and its God-given qualities will be stifled in the foul atmosphere of self.[47]

Jewels, gems and precious stones

> . . . the soul is a sign of God, a heavenly gem . . .[48]

Spiritually, human beings are like precious stones or jewels, no two alike. Some are cut and polished, while others remain in the rough. The beauty of some shines out brilliantly, while the beauty of others remains in potential only, completely hidden away.

'Abdu'l-Bahá referred to the human reality or soul as a 'depository', a receptacle inside which a unique treasure has been hidden. When this gem (the soul) is illumined by the divine light, is shaped and cut by the tests of God, and is polished by true education, it will reveal the particular and beautiful combinations of colours and qualities that are admirable purely because they were deposited there by its Creator.

> These qualifications are loved by all, for they are emanations of the father. They are the significance of his names and attributes, the direct rays of which illuminate the very essence of these qualifications.[49]

> . . . the merciful God, our Creator, has deposited within human realities certain latent and potential virtues. Through education and culture these virtues deposited by the loving God will become apparent in the

human reality, even as the unfoldment of the tree from within the germinating seed.[50]

And in the words of Bahá'u'lláh:

> Regard man as a mine rich in gems of inestimable value. Education can, alone, cause it to reveal its treasures, and enable mankind to benefit therefrom.[51]

In order to realize the beauty within, it is first necessary to recognize that this spiritual capacity exists, then to turn the mirror of the soul towards the light; otherwise this potential will not be realized.

> For an unlit candle, however great in diameter and tall, is no better than a barren palm tree or a pile of dead wood.[52]

Gradually, as humanity as a whole turns toward the knowledge of God, it too will begin to reflect the first glimmerings of spiritual civilization

> ... just as the stone, when it becomes polished and pure as a mirror, will reflect in fuller degree the glory and splendour of the sun.[53]

This chapter has looked at man's unique spiritual heritage in terms of soul, mind and spirit, which actually are just different aspects of one reality. In the next chapter, the subject of mind will be examined more closely, especially with regard to the mental faculties.

CHAPTER 8

MIND AND THE MENTAL FACULTIES

The power of the rational mind is the power of the soul over the senses.[1]

Mind is the power of the soul which expresses itself in this world through the human body.

It is a *discovering power* which apprehends things through intellectual investigation and a *directing power* which governs the physical functions of the body. Since it operates through the senses of the body, 'mind' ceases to exist as a force in this world at the moment of death. The operation of the 'common faculty' will likewise cease when the body dies. Because the outer powers no longer exist, naturally there is no further need for an intermediary agent between man's outer and inner powers. The soul, however, being an independent power that is not subject to death or decline, continues unaffected.

Mind is a discovering power

The mind is described as:

> the faculty of reasoning, by the exercise of which he is to investigate and discover the truth . . .[2]

> this power of discovery . . . this power which can grasp abstract and universal ideas . . .[3]

> the power of idealization or intellection . . .[4]

> the supreme gift of God.[5]

The following analogies are used to describe the relationship between the mind and the spirit:

> But the mind is the power of the human spirit. Spirit is the lamp; mind is the light which shines from the lamp. Spirit is the tree, and the mind is the fruit. Mind is the perfection of the spirit and is its essential quality, as the sun's rays are the essential necessity of the sun.[6]

Knowing that the operation of this amazing power is limited to the brief period of time when the soul is associated with the body is a motivation to explore it now and understand as much about it as possible.

> There is, however, a faculty in man which unfolds to his vision the secrets of existence. It gives him a power whereby he may investigate the reality of every object. It leads man on and on to the luminous station of divine sublimity and frees him from all the fetters of self, causing him to ascend to the pure heaven of sanctity. This is the power of the mind, for the soul is not, of itself, capable of unrolling the mysteries of phenomena; but the mind can accomplish this . . .[7]

Science and the mind

> There are certain pillars which have been established as the unshakeable supports of the Faith of God. The mightiest of these is learning and the use of the mind, the expansion of consciousness, and insight into the realities of the universe and the hidden mysteries of Almighty God.[8]

The great outcome of the power of the human mind is science. 'Abdu'l-Bahá called science the 'paramount virtue', and 'the first emanation from God toward man'.[9] He also said:

> It unites present and past, reveals the history of bygone nations and events, and confers upon man today the essence of all human knowledge and attainment throughout the ages. By intellectual processes and logical deductions of reason this superpower in man can penetrate the mysteries of the future and anticipate its happenings.[10]

> All the sciences and arts we now enjoy and utilize were once mysteries,

and according to the mandates of nature should have remained hidden and latent, but the human intellect has broken through the laws surrounding them and discovered the underlying realities. The mind of man has taken these mysteries out of the plane of invisibility and brought them into the plane of the known and visible.[11]

He even described science as 'the means by which man finds a pathway to God'.[12]

How could a scientist, using the amazing powers of the human mind, unfold the mysteries of the material universe and reveal the wonders of God's creation without being moved to acknowledge the existence of God?

> . . . how can I confess not to have known Thee, when, lo, the whole universe proclaimeth Thy Presence and testifieth to Thy truth?[13]

'Increase My wonder and amazement at Thee, O God!'[14]

> From that which hath been said it becometh evident that all things, in their inmost reality, testify to the revelation of the names and attributes of God within them. Each according to its capacity, indicateth, and is expressive of, the knowledge of God.[15]

Religion and science must agree

The Writings state that science and religion must agree, and that when these two forces are united, it will become the cause of the transformation of human society. There are many references on this theme.

> Religion must agree with science, so that science shall sustain religion and religion explain science. The two must be brought together, indissolubly, in reality. Down to the present day it has been customary for man to accept blindly what was called religion, even though it were not in accord with human reason.[16]

> Put all your beliefs into harmony with science; there can be no opposition, for truth is one. When religion, shorn of its superstitions, traditions, and unintelligent dogmas, shows its conformity with science, then will there be a great unifying, cleansing force in the world

which will sweep before it all wars, disagreements, discords and struggles – and then will mankind be united in the power of the Love of God.[17]

Any religious belief which is not conformable with scientific proof and investigation is superstition, for true science is reason and reality, and religion is essentially reality and pure reason; therefore, the two must correspond.[18]

The limitations of material philosophy

'Abdu'l-Bahá spent His life teaching people to become aware of the spiritual dimension and encouraging them to cultivate the spiritual qualities of the soul. Occasionally in His writings, there are passages in which He strongly condemns the attitude of the 'material philosophers' who persist in denying the existence of anything that is not perceptible to the outer senses of the body. This is one such example:

> Science exists in the mind of man as an ideal reality. The mind itself, reason itself, is an ideal reality and not tangible.
>
> Notwithstanding this, some of the sagacious men declare: We have attained to the superlative degree of knowledge; we have penetrated the laboratory of nature, studying sciences and arts; we have attained the highest station of knowledge in the human world; we have investigated the facts as they are and have arrived at the conclusion that nothing is rightly acceptable except the tangible, which alone is a reality worthy of credence; all that is not tangible is imagination and nonsense.
>
> Strange indeed that after twenty years training in colleges and universities man should reach such a station wherein he will deny the existence of the ideal or that which is not perceptible to the senses. Have you ever stopped to think that the animal already has graduated from such a university? Have you ever realized that the cow is already a professor emeritus of that university? For the cow without hard labour and study is already a philosopher of the superlative degree in the school of nature. The cow denies everything that is not tangible, saying, 'I can see! I can eat! Therefore, I believe only in that which is tangible!'
>
> Then why should we go to the colleges? Let us go to the cow.[19]

Material science and divine science: Wings of man's upliftment

Material science and divine science are like two wings of upliftment, and man is called upon to develop both. To cling to religion only will result in superstition; to cling to science only is to risk becoming engrossed in the material world.

> Scientific knowledge is the highest attainment upon the human plane, for science is the discoverer of realities. It is of two kinds: material and spiritual. Material science is the investigation of natural phenomena; divine science is the discovery and realization of spiritual verities. The world of humanity must acquire both. A bird has two wings; it cannot fly with one. Material and spiritual science are the two wings of human uplift and attainment. Both are necessary – one the natural, the other supernatural; one material, the other divine. By the divine we mean the discovery of the mysteries of God, the comprehension of spiritual realities, the wisdom of God, inner significances of the heavenly religions and foundation of the law.[20]

> Religion and science are the two wings upon which man's intelligence can soar into the heights, with which the human soul can progress. It is not possible to fly with one wing alone! Should a man try to fly with the wing of religion alone he would quickly fall into the quagmire of superstition, whilst on the other hand, with the wing of science alone he would also make no progress, but fall into the despairing slough of materialism. All religions of the present day have fallen into superstitious practices, out of harmony alike with the true principles of the teaching they represent and with the scientific discoveries of the time. Many religious leaders have grown to think that the importance of religion lies mainly in the adherence to a collection of certain dogmas and the practice of rites and ceremonies! Those whose souls they profess to cure are taught to believe likewise, and these cling tenaciously to the outward forms, confusing them with the inward truth.[21]

Weigh all things in this balance

> It is impossible for religion to be contrary to science, even though some intellects are too weak or too immature to understand truth.

God made religion and science to be the measure, as it were, of our understanding. Take heed that you neglect not such a wonderful power. Weigh all things in this balance.[22]

The fruit of science

The fruit of every science should be the love of God.

> With the love of God all sciences are accepted and beloved, but without it, are fruitless; nay, rather the cause of insanity. Every science is like unto a tree; if the fruit of it is the love of God, that is a blessed tree. Otherwise it is dried wood and finally a food for fire.[23]

If material science alone is developed without regard to divine science, dire consequences are predicted.

> The civilization, so often vaunted by the learned exponents of arts and sciences, will, if allowed to overleap the bounds of moderation, bring great evil upon men. Thus warneth you He Who is the All-Knowing. If carried to excess, civilization will prove as prolific a source of evil as it had been of goodness when kept within the restraints of moderation.[24]

> Whatsoever passeth beyond the limits of moderation will cease to exert a beneficial influence. Consider for instance such things as liberty, civilization and the like. However much men of understanding may favourably regard them, they will, if carried to excess, exercise a pernicious influence upon men . . .[25]

'Sensible' existences and 'intellectual' existences

Mind is a power which perceives intellectual realities.

> The sciences, arts, inventions, trades and discoveries of realities are the results of this spiritual power. This is a power which encompasses all things, comprehends their realities, discovers all the hidden mysteries of beings, and through this knowledge controls them. It even perceives things which do not exist outwardly – that is to say, intellectual realities which are not sensible, and which have no outward existence because

they are invisible; so it comprehends the mind, the spirit, the qualities, the characters, the love and sorrow of man, which are intellectual realities.[26]

The words 'sensible' and 'intellectual' are explained in these terms:

> Things which are sensible are those which are perceived by the five exterior senses; thus those outward existences which the eyes see are called sensible. Intellectual things are those which have no outward existence but are conceptions of the mind. For example, mind itself is an intellectual thing which has no outward existence. All man's characteristics and qualities form an intellectual existence and are not sensible.
>
> Briefly, the intellectual realities, such as all the qualities and admirable perfections of man, are purely good, and exist. Evil is simply their nonexistence. So ignorance is the want of knowledge; error is the want of guidance; forgetfulness is the want of memory; stupidity is the want of good sense. All these things have no real existence.[27]

Where is the mind and spirit?

'Abdu'l-Bahá says that the 'mind' 'is connected with the acquisition of knowledge'[28] and that it is connected with the brain, but this is not a physical or measurable association. Dissect the brain, and you will not find the mind.

> The mind which is in man, the existence of which is recognized – where is it in him? If you examine the body with the eye, the ear or the other senses, you will not find it; nevertheless, it exists. Therefore, the mind has no place, but it is connected with the brain. The Kingdom is also like this. In the same way love has no place, but it is connected with the heart; so the Kingdom has no place, but is connected with man.[29]

> Intelligence does not partake of the quality of space, though it is related to man's brain. The intellect resides there, but not materially. Search in the brain you will not find the intellect. In the same way, though the soul is a resident of the body it is not to be found in the body.[30]

The spirit surrounds the body. The mind and spirit give awareness of the physical body and of powers, feelings and spiritual conditions.

For example, the mind and the spirit of man are cognizant of the conditions and states of the members and component parts of the body, and are aware of all the physical sensations; in the same way, they are aware of their power, of their feelings, and of their spiritual conditions. This is the knowledge of being which man realizes and perceives, for the spirit surrounds the body and is aware of its sensations and powers. This knowledge is not the outcome of effort and study. It is an existing thing; it is an absolute gift.[31]

Body is essential to mind

Mind is the result or fruit of the soul expressing its power through the body; therefore, if the body is unsound, the mind will reflect that imperfection. This is why 'Abdu'l-Bahá states that the power of the mind cannot be manifested without the body – it is dependent upon the sound functioning of the human body. The light inside a lamp may continue to shine brightly, but if the lamp is covered in grime, the amount of light escaping will be greatly diminished.

> Consider how the human intellect develops and weakens, and may at times come to naught, whereas the soul changeth not. For the mind to manifest itself, the human body must be whole; and a sound mind cannot be but in a sound body, whereas the soul dependeth not upon the body. It is through the power of the soul that the mind comprehendeth, imagineth and exerteth its influence, whilst the soul is a power that is free. The mind comprehendeth the abstract by the aid of the concrete, but the soul hath limitless manifestations of its own. The mind is circumscribed, the soul limitless. It is by the aid of such senses as those of sight, hearing, taste, smell and touch, that the mind comprehendeth, whereas, the soul is free from all agencies . . . The mind, moreover, understandeth not whilst the senses have ceased to function . . .[32]

The soul is not affected by sickness of the body, but the mind is

If the body becomes sick for whatever reason, the mind may be affected, but the soul will remain unaffected. Sickness and infirmity of the body will never affect the soul.

> Know thou that the soul of man is exalted above, and is independent of all infirmities of body or mind.³³

Mind is a potent force associated with this world; it is the fruit which comes out of the association of the spiritual (the soul) with the physical (the human body). Sometimes the expression of that mind force is severely limited due to sickness or to particular conditions which handicap the body. In such cases it may appear that the person's mental faculties are non-existent, whereas in reality these faculties exist, but are prevented from being expressed due to the disability.

> The temple of man is like unto a mirror, his soul is as the sun, and his mental faculties even as the rays that emanate from that source of light. The ray may cease to fall upon the mirror, but it can in no wise be dissociated from the sun.³⁴

It sometimes happens that healthy people of sound mind make choices which lead not only to physical sicknesses but also to the disintegration of their minds. One of the few times that Bahá'u'lláh specifically mentions some material thing having the power to affect the soul is when He refers to the use of certain substances.³⁵ 'Abdu'l-Bahá comments:

> For opium fasteneth on the soul so that the user's conscience dieth, his mind is blotted away, his perceptions are eroded. It turneth the living into the dead. It quencheth the natural heat. No greater harm can be conceived than that which opium inflicteth. Fortunate are they who never even speak the name of it; then think how wretched is the user . . .
>
> Alcohol consumeth the mind and causeth man to commit acts of absurdity, but this opium, this foul fruit of the infernal tree, and this wicked hashish extinguish the mind, freeze the spirit, petrify the soul, waste the body and leave man frustrated and lost.³⁶

Mind is the agency which directs the body

In the following Tablet, 'Abdu'l-Bahá draws a parallel between the 'universal power' directing and regulating the infinite universe, and the mind which directs and co-ordinates the various functions of the human body.

The mind force – whether we call it pre-existent or contingent – doth direct and co-ordinate all the members of the human body, seeing to it that each part or member duly performeth its own special function. If, however, there be some interruption in the power of the mind, all the members will fail to carry out their essential functions, deficiencies will appear in the body and the functioning of its members, and the power will prove ineffective.

Likewise, look into this endless universe: a universal power inevitably existeth, which encompasseth all, directing and regulating all the parts of this infinite creation; and were it not for this Director, this Co-ordinator, the universe would be flawed and deficient. It would be even as a madman; whereas ye can see that this endless creation carrieth out its functions in perfect order, every separate part of it performing its own task with complete reliability, nor is there any flaw to be found in all its workings. Thus it is clear that a Universal Power existeth, directing and regulating this infinite universe. Every rational mind can grasp this fact.[37]

The same theme is re-stated in 'Abdu'l-Bahá's Tablet to Dr Auguste Forel[38] where He describes the operation of 'mind' in the human kingdom as the expression of a spiritual power which brings order, unity and harmony to the various functions of the human body.

Consider the body of man, and let the part be an indication of the whole. Consider how these diverse parts and members of the human body are closely connected and harmoniously united one with the other. Every part is the essential requisite of all other parts and has a function by itself. It is the mind that is the all-unifying agency that so uniteth all the component parts one with the other that each dischargeth its specific function in perfect order, and thereby co-operation and reaction are made possible. All parts function under certain laws that are essential to existence. Should that all-unifying agency that directeth all these parts be harmed in any way there is no doubt that the constituent parts and members will cease functioning properly; and though that all-unifying agency in the temple of man be not sensed or seen and the reality thereof be unknown, yet by its effects it manifesteth itself with the greatest power . . .

For instance, as we have observed, co-operation among the

constituent parts of the human body is clearly established, and these parts and members render services unto all the component parts of the body. For instance, the hand, the foot, the eye, the ear, the mind, the imagination all help the various parts and members of the human body, but all these interactions are linked by an unseen, all-embracing power, that causeth these interactions to be produced with perfect regularity. This is the inner faculty of man, that is his spirit and his mind, both of which are invisible.[39]

Science is worship and art is a service to the kingdom of God

All sciences, knowledge, arts, wonders, institutions, discoveries and enterprises come from the exercised intelligence of the rational soul. There was a time when they were unknown, preserved mysteries and hidden secrets; the rational soul gradually discovered them and brought them out from the plane of the invisible and the hidden into the realm of the visible.[40]

If a man engageth with all his power in the acquisition of a science or in the perfection of an art, it is as if he has been worshipping God in churches and temples. Thus as thou enterest a school of agriculture and strivest in the acquisition of that science thou art day and night engaged in acts of worship – acts that are accepted at the threshold of the Almighty. What bounty greater than this that science should be considered as an act of worship and art as service to the Kingdom of God.[41]

Achievements in the field of the arts and the sciences do not come easily; they require real effort. The same principle applies to the potential of the human mind. The gap between an ignorant person and a wise person relates to the degree to which the powers of the mind have been unfolded.

The intrinsic difference between the ignorant man and the astute philosopher is that the former has not been lifted out of his natural condition, while the latter has undergone systematic training and education in schools and colleges until his mind has awakened and unfolded to higher realms of thought and perception . . .[42]

Every person must be given the opportunity to learn some science and philosophy.

> No individual should be denied or deprived of intellectual training, although each should receive according to capacity. None must be left in the grades of ignorance, for ignorance is a defect in the human world. All mankind must be given a knowledge of science and philosophy – that is, as much as may be deemed necessary. All cannot be scientists and philosophers, but each should be educated according to his needs and deserts.[43]

Science is the love of reality

'Abdu'l-Bahá called science 'the love of reality'[44] and further declared:

> The Prophets of God have been the servants of reality; Their teachings constitute the science of reality.[45]

The knowledge revealed by the Messengers of God enhances man's spiritual capacity, and it also provides the basis for man's understanding of the phenomenal world. The potential for the various sciences to continue advancing, by revealing new wonders in God's creation, is limitless. On that basis, therefore, the evolving nature of scientific discovery must eventually bring science and religion closer together until finally it will be recognized that they are one, that truth is one. In the meantime,

> ... our whole approach to each matter is based on the belief that God sends us divinely inspired Educators; what they tell us is fundamentally true; what science tells us today is true, tomorrow may be entirely changed to better explain a new set of facts. [46]

The two most luminous lights

In this section the powers of the human rational soul have been examined by referring predominantly to the writings of 'Abdu'l-Bahá, so it seems fitting to conclude this chapter by using His words as quoted on the opening page of His book *The Secret of Divine Civilization*:

In the Name of God the Clement, the Merciful

Praise and thanksgiving be unto Providence that out of all the realities in existence He has chosen the reality of man and has honoured it with intellect and wisdom, the two most luminous lights in either world. Through the agency of this great endowment, He has in every epoch cast on the mirror of creation new and wonderful configurations. If we look objectively upon the world of being, it will become apparent that from age to age, the temple of existence has continually been embellished with a fresh grace, and distinguished with an ever-varying splendour, deriving from wisdom and the power of thought.

This supreme emblem of God stands first in the order of creation and first in rank, taking precedence over all created things. Witness to it is the Holy Tradition, 'Before all else, God created the mind.' From the dawn of creation, it was made to be revealed in the temple of man.[47]

CHAPTER 9

THE STRUGGLE WITHIN

If the search for truth is successful, then the spirit of faith is born in man, but the transformation of character involves an inner struggle which continues throughout this life.

Self, ego and man's lower nature

> This lower nature in man is symbolized as Satan – the evil ego within us, not an evil personality outside.[1]

The force of gravity has a spiritual equivalent in man, namely his lower nature, 'the centre of self'.

> Just as the earth attracts everything to the centre of gravity, and every object thrown upward into space will come down, so also material ideas and worldly thoughts attract man to the centre of self. Anger, passion, ignorance, prejudice, greed, envy, covetousness, jealousy and suspicion prevent man from ascending to the realms of holiness, imprisoning him in the claws of self and the cage of egotism. The physical man, unassisted by the divine power, trying to escape from one of these invisible enemies, will unconsciously fall into the hands of another. No sooner does he attempt to soar upward than the density of the love of self, like the power of gravity, draws him to the earth. The only power that is capable of delivering man from this captivity is the power of the breaths of the Holy Spirit.[2]

The love of self is a great threat to spiritual growth; it is a force which will pull man down if he neglects such things as prayer, meditation, reading the Word of God and acting in harmony with the divine teachings. These are the habits which will keep him from being captured in the 'cage of egotism'. The daily recital of prayers, especially those revealed by the Messenger of God, is an effective way of keeping the ego in check. Throughout all these prayers are beautiful passages which call forth attitudes of humility and self-effacement in the individual, as the following excerpts reveal:

> I bear witness at this moment, O my God, to my helplessness and Thy sovereignty, my feebleness and Thy power. I know not that which profiteth me or harmeth me . . .[3]

> Thou before Whose wisdom the wise falleth short and faileth, before Whose knowledge the learned confesseth his ignorance, before Whose might the strong waxeth weak, before Whose wealth the rich testifieth to his poverty, before Whose light the enlightened is lost in darkness, toward the shrine of Whose knowledge turneth the essence of all understanding and around the sanctuary of Whose presence circle the souls of all mankind.[4]

If man neglects his spiritual development and instead chooses to gratify his lower nature, he will become trapped:

> Ye are even as the bird which soareth, with the full force of its mighty wings and with complete and joyous confidence, through the immensity of the heavens, until, impelled to satisfy its hunger, it turneth longingly to the water and clay of the earth below it, and, having been entrapped in the mesh of its desire, findeth itself impotent to resume its flight to the realms whence it came. Powerless to shake off the burden weighing on its sullied wings, that bird, hitherto an inmate of the heavens, is now forced to seek a dwelling-place upon the dust.[5]

The soul 'emanates' from the worlds of God. When it grows and develops in a spiritual sense, the soul recognizes its separation from God, and yearns for the Kingdom of God in both this world and the next.

> O thou spiritual friend! This world is a prison for heavenly souls, and this earthly world is but a cage, and not a nest, unto the divine birds . . . When the heart becometh free from attachment unto this world, it will crave for the world of the Kingdom and seek for eternal life.[6]

God's claim on the human heart

The heart can become attracted to any number of different things which may draw it away from God, but this will result in a sense of emptiness, because He (the Creator) has laid claim on the human heart, and when man turns away from God, he is turning away from the opportunity to fulfil the purpose for which he was created.

The Messenger of God establishes that prior claim on man in the most emphatic language:

> Our mission is to seize and possess the hearts of men.[7]

> The one true God, exalted be His glory, hath ever regarded, and will continue to regard, the hearts of men as His own, His exclusive possession.[8]

His mystical work Hidden Words contains numerous references to this theme:

> O Son of Dust! All that is in heaven and earth I have ordained for thee, except the human heart, which I have made the habitation of My beauty and glory . . .[9]

> O Son of Being! Thy heart is My home; sanctify it for My descent. Thy spirit is My place of revelation; cleanse it for My manifestation.[10]

He warns that the heart cannot be attached to this world and love God at the same time. Man must choose.

> O Son of Earth! Wouldst thou have Me, seek none other than Me; and wouldst thou gaze upon My beauty, close thine eyes to the world and all that is therein; for My will and the will of another than Me, even as fire and water, cannot dwell together in one heart.[11]

When the love of God *does* appear in the heart, this makes it possible for other divine bounties to be revealed.

> . . . for the greatest bestowal of God is love. Love is the source of all

the bestowals of God. Until love takes possession of the heart no other divine bounty can be revealed in it.[12]

The Messengers of God have the key to the human heart; They appear in order to uncover the pathway leading to divine knowledge; They reveal the Word of God, the power which has dominion over the hearts of men.

> The Word is the master key for the whole world, inasmuch as through its potency the doors of the hearts of men, which in reality are the doors of heaven, are unlocked.[13]

Life is a struggle

While the lower nature in man pulls him towards the world, the higher nature draws him in the opposite direction, towards the spiritual world. These opposing tendencies in man produce the tensions which characterize the struggle of life; they define his essential challenge in this world, namely, trying to live according to spiritual principles while simultaneously resisting the pull of his material nature.

> Effort is an inseparable part of man's life. It may take different forms with the changing conditions of the world, but it will be always present as a necessary element in our earthly existence. Life is after all a struggle. Progress is attained through struggle, and without such a struggle life ceases to have a meaning; it becomes even extinct.[14]

If there were no such struggle, the journey of the soul would not be necessary.

> Briefly, the journey of the soul is necessary. The pathway of life is the road which leads to divine knowledge and attainment. Without training and guidance the soul could never progress beyond the conditions of its lower nature which is ignorant and defective.[15]

Man in his natural state is imperfect

> If man himself is left in his natural state, he will become lower than the animal and continue to grow more ignorant and imperfect . . . If

we wish to illumine this dark plane of human existence, we must bring man forth from the hopeless captivity of nature . . .[16]

From the beginning, man is in a state of imperfection, abiding between the physical nature and the spiritual nature. He needs to acquire perfections. 'Abdu'l-Bahá says that the reality of man stands 'between the world of the animal and the world of Divinity'.[17]

> The physical nature is inherited from Adam, and the spiritual nature is inherited from the Reality of the Word of God... is born from the bounty of the Holy Spirit. The first is the source of all imperfection; the second is the source of all perfection.[18]

It is the nature of the human heart to love; if it does not love God, it will love the things of the world. Left alone, man will naturally attach himself to the world. The material nature is his 'default' setting, as it were. Therefore, to free himself from the conditions of that nature will require effort. Yet he cannot do this unaided; he requires divine assistance.

> The holy Manifestations of God come into the world to dispel the darkness of the animal, or physical, nature of man, to purify him from his imperfections in order that his heavenly and spiritual nature may become quickened, his divine qualities awakened, his perfections visible, his potential powers revealed and all the virtues of the world of humanity latent within him may come to life. These holy Manifestations of God are the Educators and Trainers of the world of existence, the Teachers of the world of humanity. They liberate man from the darkness of the world of nature, deliver him from despair, error, ignorance, imperfections and all evil qualities. They clothe him in the garment of perfections and exalted virtues. Men are ignorant; the Manifestations of God make them wise. They are animalistic; the Manifestations make them human. They are savage and cruel; the Manifestations lead them into kingdoms of light and love. They are unjust; the Manifestations cause them to become just. Man is selfish; they sever him from self and desire. Man is haughty; They make him meek, humble and friendly. He is earthly; They make him heavenly. Men are material; the Manifestations transform them into divine semblance. They are immature children; the Manifestations develop them into maturity. Man is poor;

they endow him with wealth. Man is base, treacherous and mean; the
Manifestations of God uplift him into dignity, nobility and loftiness.[19]

It is one of the great paradoxes that man, although being imperfect and living in an imperfect world, is nevertheless here for the sole purpose of striving for unattainable perfection. Absolute perfection belongs to God only. Man on the other hand, while limited, has an enormous potential, and once spiritually awakened, is able to advance in both the material and spiritual sense.

> . . . human perfections are infinite. Thus, however learned a man may be, we can imagine one more learned.[20]

> As the divine bounties are endless, so human perfections are endless.[21]

> The wisdom of the appearance of the spirit in the body is this: the human spirit is a Divine Trust, and it must traverse all conditions, for its passage and movement through the conditions of existence will be the means of its acquiring perfections.[22]

John Bunyan's famous book *Pilgrim's Progress* is a narrative based upon just such a scenario, namely, a journey of testing leading to the acquiring of spiritual perfections in preparation for entrance into the Kingdom of God. This story about a pilgrim's personal tests is equally a story about choice.

The power of choice

Although man may have free will, it is a power which is limited to personal actions and behaviours. Essentially, it is a power of moral choice. Most of the other elements of life are beyond man's control and many are things which cannot even be anticipated, such as health scares, accidents, whether or not transport arrives or leaves on time, the impact of other people's actions, and so on.

> Some things are subject to the free will of man, such as justice, equity, tyranny and injustice, in other words, good and evil actions; it is evident and clear that these actions are, for the most part, left to the will of man. But there are certain things to which man is forced and compelled, such as sleep, death, sickness, decline of power, injuries and

> misfortunes; these are not subject to the will of man, and he is not responsible for them, for he is compelled to endure them. But in the choice of good and bad actions he is free, and he commits them according to his own will.
>
> For example, if he wishes, he can pass his time in praising God, or he can be occupied with other thoughts. He can be an enkindled light through the fire of the love of God, and a philanthropist loving the world, or he can be a hater of mankind, and engrossed with material things. He can be just or cruel. These actions and these deeds are subject to the control of the will of man himself; consequently, he is responsible for them.[23]

The freedom to make choices lies at the heart of what it is to be human, and exercising that power gives meaning to this life; however, as the line between right and wrong in human behaviour has become increasingly blurred, this power of choice has been correspondingly diminished. As the teaching of moral values has declined in society, so have attitudes towards antisocial behaviour changed. Someone who commits a crime is looked upon less as one who has chosen to harm society and more as a victim of negative social circumstances. Criminals are referred for an assessment of their psychological or mental health, as if the discovery of some form of psychological imbalance might explain their behaviour. It cannot be denied that many people may not have received a strong moral education, but to encourage the view that they do not or cannot know right from wrong and are therefore unable to exercise their power of choice amounts to dehumanizing them; it is a denial of their higher spiritual nature.

Taking away man's responsibility for his actions removes all the constraints on his behaviour, and when the principles of reward and punishment in society are increasingly eroded, it results in the kind of liberty which Bahá'u'lláh warned will 'infringe on the dignity of his station'.[24]

If there were no right or wrong, then the power of choice would be pointless. The importance of exercising that power and choosing correctly directly influences the security of society, the spiritual condition of society, and also the life of the individual here and in the world to come.

> In man there are two natures; his spiritual or higher nature and his material or lower nature. In one he approaches God, in the other he lives for the world alone. Signs of both these natures are to be found

in men. In his material aspect he expresses untruth, cruelty and injustice; all these are the outcome of his lower nature. The attributes of his Divine nature are shown forth in love, mercy, kindness, truth and justice, one and all being expressions of his higher nature. Every good habit, every noble quality belongs to man's spiritual nature, whereas all his imperfections and sinful actions are born of his material nature.[25]

If the soul identifies itself with the material world it remains dark, for in the natural world there is corruption, aggression, struggles for existence, greed, darkness, transgression and vice. If the soul remains in this station and moves along these paths it will be the recipient of this darkness; but if it becomes the recipient of the graces of the world of mind, its darkness will be transformed into light, its tyranny into justice, its ignorance into wisdom, its aggression into loving kindness; until it reach the apex. Then there will not remain any struggle for existence. Man will become free from egotism; he will be released from the material world . . .[26]

Attachment to the material world

No matter how 'spiritual' a person is, living in a material world means having to deal with material things. Activities such as earning money, buying, selling, owning property, acquiring assets and taking care of one's family are necessary, and, for most, unavoidable facts of life. Wealth is neither negative nor positive – it is simply an element of this material existence; however, it is easy to become attached to wealth and the idea of having wealth, and such attachment can hinder man's spiritual progress.

> Should a man wish to adorn himself with the ornaments of the earth, to wear its apparels, or partake of the benefits it can bestow, no harm can befall him, if he alloweth nothing whatever to intervene between him and God, for God hath ordained every good thing, whether created in the heavens or in the earth, for such of His servants as truly believe in Him.[27]

In the New Testament, the same principle is expressed by the Apostle Paul; he does not say that *money* is evil, he only warns against the heart becoming attached to it:

For the love of money is the root of all evil . . .[28]

The challenge that this presents to man is to live in this material world while at the same time focusing his thoughts on the next world. Adib Taherzadeh illustrates this principle in one of his books:

> To give an example: we note a great similarity between the laws governing the life of a tree and those which motivate the life of man, both physically and spiritually. We note that the tree thrusts its roots deep into the soil and draws on the minerals in the earth for its food. The soil is inferior to the tree; the tree is nevertheless dependent upon it for its existence. In spite of this dependence, the tree grows in the opposite direction, away from the soil. As if disliking the soil, it raises up its branches high towards the sky. This is similar to man and his state of detachment from the material world when his soul aspires to spiritual things and renounces earthly desires.[29]

Man strives after material things because of the belief that they will give him freedom and happiness, yet the opposite is true; if he fails to detach himself from these things, then he will almost certainly become completely entangled in his desires and bring unnecessary pain and grief upon himself. Those who believe that wealth will protect them from the uncertainty of life, and treasure their health for no other reason than to prolong the physical life, have failed to realize the real purpose of life.

> Luxuries cut off the freedom of communication. One who is imprisoned by desires is always unhappy; the children of the Kingdom have unchained themselves from their desires. Break all fetters and seek for spiritual joy and enlightenment; then, though you walk on this earth, you will perceive yourselves to be within the divine horizon. To man alone is this possible.[30]

To chase after the things of this world will produce as much reward as chasing after a shadow.

> The world is but a show, vain and empty, a mere nothing, bearing the semblance of reality. Set not your affections upon it. Break not the bond that uniteth you with your Creator . . .[31]

> Know thou that the Kingdom is the real world, and this nether place is only its shadow stretching out. A shadow hath no life of its own; its existence is only a fantasy, and nothing more; it is but images reflected in water, and seeming as pictures to the eye.[32]

The station of those who pride themselves on the possession of perishable things is deemed to be lower than even the mineral kingdom, since it is clear that all these things come from the earth itself by God's mercy, and this knowledge should lead man to show humility.

> What is it of which ye can rightly boast? Is it on your food and your drink that ye pride yourselves, on the riches ye lay up in your treasuries, on the diversity and the cost of the ornaments with which ye deck yourselves? If true glory were to consist in the possession of such perishable things, then the earth on which ye walk must needs vaunt itself over you, because it supplieth you, and bestoweth upon you, these very things, by the decree of the Almighty. In its bowels are contained, according to what God hath ordained, all that ye possess. From it, as a sign of His mercy, ye derive your riches. Behold then your state, the thing in which ye glory! Would that ye could perceive it![33]

> Soon will your swiftly-passing days be over, and the fame and riches, the comforts, the joys provided by this rubbish-heap, the world, will be gone without a trace.[34]

The principle that 'attachment leads to loss'

> What result is forthcoming from material rest, tranquillity, luxury and attachment to this corporeal world! It is evident that the man who pursues these things will in the end become afflicted with regret and loss.[35]

In the material world man attaches himself to something in order to feel more secure, or so as not to lose it; whereas Bahá'u'lláh warns that those who seek security in, or who pride themselves in, their possessions or their learning ultimately lose everything, since all the things connected with this world are transitory and will eventually completely disappear.

> Those men who, having amassed the vanities and ornaments of the earth, have turned away disdainfully from God – these have lost both this world and the world to come. Ere long, will God, with the Hand of Power, strip them of their possessions, and divest them of the robe of His bounty.[36]

> Whither are gone the learned men, the divines and potentates of old? What hath become of their discriminating views, their shrewd perceptions, their subtle insights and sage pronouncements? Where are their hidden coffers, their flaunted ornaments, their gilded couches, their rugs and cushions strewn about? Gone forever is their generation! All have perished, and, by God's decree, naught remaineth of them but scattered dust. Exhausted is the wealth they gathered, dispersed the stores they hoarded, dissipated the treasures they concealed. Naught can now be seen but their deserted haunts, their roofless dwellings, their uprooted tree-trunks, and their faded splendour. No man of insight will let wealth distract his gaze from his ultimate objective, and no man of understanding will allow riches to withhold him from turning unto Him Who is the All-Possessing, the Most High.[37]

The principle of temporary ownership

No matter how much we own and acquire, sooner or later it must be conceded that these things will pass from us. Accepting this principle makes it easier to regard material possessions with some degree of detachment.

> Say: Rejoice not in the things ye possess; tonight they are yours, tomorrow others will possess them. Thus warneth you He Who is the All-Knowing, the All-Informed. Say: Can ye claim that what ye own is lasting or secure? Nay! . . . The days of your life flee away as a breath of wind, and all your pomp and glory shall be folded up as were the pomp and glory of those gone before you.[38]

> Others ere long will lay hands on what ye possess, and enter into your habitations. Incline your ears to My words, and be not numbered among the foolish.[39]

The senselessness of acquiring material things for their own sake is summed up in this verse from the New Testament: 'For we brought nothing into this world, and it is certain we can carry nothing out.'⁴⁰

It is ironic that man acquires material things with a view to making himself more comfortable in this world when actually he is in the process of leaving it.

> Say: If ye be seekers after this life and the vanities thereof, ye should have sought them while ye were still enclosed in your mothers' wombs, for at that time ye were continually approaching them, could ye but perceive it. Ye have, on the other hand, ever since ye were born and attained maturity, been all the while receding from the world and drawing closer to dust. Why, then, exhibit such greed in amassing the treasures of the earth, when your days are numbered and your chance is well-nigh lost?⁴¹

CHAPTER 10

TO SEEK AND TO FIND

All those who seek truth in the Heavenly Kingdom shine like the stars; they are like fruit trees laden with choice fruit, like seas full of precious pearls.[1]

The principle of discovering truth for oneself

... every man hath been, and will continue to be, able of himself to appreciate the Beauty of God, the Glorified. Had he not been endowed with such a capacity, how could he be called to account for his failure?[2]

In order to find truth we must give up our prejudices, our own small trivial notions; an open receptive mind is essential. If our chalice is full of self, there is no room in it for the water of life. The fact that we imagine ourselves to be right and everybody else wrong is the greatest of all obstacles in the path towards unity, and unity is necessary if we would reach truth, for truth is *one*.

Therefore it is imperative that we should renounce our own particular prejudices and superstitions if we earnestly desire to seek the truth. Unless we make a distinction in our minds between dogma, superstition and prejudice on the one hand, and truth on the other, we cannot succeed. When we are in earnest in our search for anything we look for it everywhere. This principle we must carry out in our search for truth.

Science must be accepted. No one truth can contradict another truth. Light is good in whatsoever lamp it is burning! A rose is beautiful in whatsoever garden it may bloom! A star has the same radiance if it shines from the East or from the West. Be free from prejudice, so will you love the Sun of Truth from whatsoever point in the horizon it may arise! You will realize that if the Divine light of truth shone in Jesus Christ it also shone in Moses and in Buddha. The earnest seeker will arrive at this truth. This is what is meant by the 'Search after Truth'.

It means, also, that we must be willing to clear away all that we have previously learned, all that would clog our steps on the way to truth; we must not shrink if necessary from beginning our education all over again. We must not allow our love for any one religion or any one personality to so blind our eyes that we become fettered by superstition! When we are freed from all these bonds, seeking with liberated minds, then shall we be able to arrive at our goal.

'Seek the truth, the truth shall make you free.' So shall we see the truth in all religions, for truth is in all and truth is one![3]

> He must so cleanse his heart that no remnant of either love or hate may linger therein, lest that love blindly incline him to error, or that hate repel him away from the truth.[4]

The seeker's effort will be rewarded

The following words of encouragement to the spiritual seeker are from the Old Testament:

> And ye shall seek me, and find me, when ye shall search for me with all your heart.[5]

In the New Testament a similar promise is contained in the words of Christ:

> And I say unto you, Ask, and it shall be given you; seek, and ye shall find; knock, and it shall be opened unto you.
> For every one that asketh receiveth; and he that seeketh findeth; and to him that knocketh it shall be opened.[6]

This spiritual assurance is associated with the revelation of every Messenger of God. The same promise is repeated in the Bahá'í Writings in various passages, for example:

> The more a man seeketh light from the Sun of Truth, the nearer he will draw.[7]

> He hath extended assistance to every wayfarer, hath graciously responded to every petitioner and granted admittance to every seeker after truth.[8]
>
> For far be it from His greatness and His glory that He should turn away a seeker at His door, cast aside from His Threshold one who hath set his hopes on Him, reject one who hath sought the shelter of His shade, deprive one who hath held fast to the hem of His mercy, or condemn to remoteness the poor one who hath found the river of His riches.[9]
>
> Thou disappointest no one who hath sought Thee, nor dost Thou keep back from Thee any one who hath desired Thee.[10]

The following excerpts taken from the prayers of Bahá'u'lláh are especially relevant to the seeker:

> Cast not away, O my Lord, him that hath turned towards Thee, nor suffer him who hath drawn nigh unto Thee to be removed far from Thy court. Dash not the hopes of the suppliant who hath longingly stretched out his hands to seek Thy grace and favours, and deprive not Thy sincere servants of the wonders of Thy tender mercies and loving-kindness.[11]
>
> O My God! Thou art the All-Bountiful, Whose grace is infinite. Withhold not Thy servants from the most mighty Ocean, which Thou hast made the repository of the pearls of Thy knowledge and Thy wisdom, and turn them not away from Thy gate, which Thou hast opened wide before all who are in Thy heaven and all who are on Thy earth.[12]

The bird of the spirit

When the soul is illumined by the light of the love of God it will break free from the captivity of the material world and its imperfections, and soar.

> O Son of Spirit! Burst thy cage asunder, and even as the phoenix of love soar into the firmament of holiness. Renounce thyself and, filled with the spirit of mercy, abide in the realm of celestial sanctity.[13]

This analogy of the soul as a bird rising above the mortal world on the wings of the love of God is also touched upon in the Old Testament:

> But they that wait upon the Lord shall renew their strength; they shall mount up with wings as eagles; they shall run, and not be weary; and they shall walk, and not faint.[14]

For a person who has not been brought up to believe in God, or who has previously been a blind follower observing the outward form of a religion due to family belief or tradition, that mystical moment when the light of spiritual understanding begins to flood into the soul can be an uplifting, exhilarating experience. Bahá'u'lláh refers to 'the trumpet-blast of knowledge' awakening the heart, soul and spirit of the seeker who He says will then, gazing with the eye of inner vision, come to see the hand of God in everything.

> Only when the lamp of search, of earnest striving, of longing desire, of passionate devotion, of fervid love, of rapture, and ecstasy, is kindled within the seeker's heart, and the breeze of His loving-kindness is wafted upon his soul, will the darkness of error be dispelled, the mists of doubts and misgivings be dissipated, and the lights of knowledge and certitude envelop his being. At that hour will the mystic Herald, bearing the joyful tidings of the Spirit, shine forth from the City of God resplendent as the morn, and, through the trumpet-blast of knowledge, will awaken the heart, the soul, and the spirit from the slumber of negligence. Then will the manifold favours and outpouring grace of the holy and everlasting Spirit confer such new life upon the seeker that he will find himself endowed with a new eye, a new ear, a new heart, and a new mind. He will contemplate the manifest signs of the universe, and will penetrate the hidden mysteries of the soul. Gazing with the eye of God, he will perceive within every atom a door that leadeth him to the stations of absolute certitude. He will discover in all things the mysteries of divine Revelation and the evidences of an everlasting manifestation.[15]

Like lightning

Throughout the Writings, we find many statements which associate 'light' with the beginning of spiritual understanding. In the following quotation 'Abdu'l-Bahá extends this analogy by relating the appearance of the

Messenger of God in this world to 'lightning', one of the most powerful manifestations of light and energy in the physical world.

> But through Thy greatest bounty, the glorious dawn broke and the lightning of guidance flashed from the Supreme Horizon upon the face of heaven![16]

How appropriate that the flash of intense light in the midst of an electrical storm should have as its spiritual parallel the appearance of God's bounty and guidance to mankind. Similarly, the moment in which a soul realizes and discovers its connection to God can be intensely illuminating, even electrifying in its effect on that individual.

This gift of spiritual illumination can be attained in an instant because the ocean of the knowledge of God is very close. Bahá'u'lláh writes:

> This most great, this fathomless and surging Ocean is near, astonishingly near, unto you. Behold it is closer to you than your life-vein! Swift as the twinkling of an eye ye can, if ye but wish it, reach and partake of this imperishable favour, this God-given grace, this incorruptible gift, this most potent and unspeakably glorious bounty.[17]

> Take thou the step of the spirit, so that, swift as the twinkling of an eye, thou mayest flash through the wilds of remoteness . . . and in one breath commune with the heavenly Spirits.[18]

He uses similar language when referring to spiritual seekers who have already made that connection:

> For these have passed over the worlds of names, and fled beyond the worlds of attributes as swift as lightning.[19]

These statements reveal how rapidly a person's character can be transformed when the soul is affected by the power of the Word of God.

The Divine Elixir

The catalyst which brings about this transformation in the human spirit is referred to in the Writings as the 'Divine Elixir':

> Likewise, these souls, through the potency of the Divine Elixir, traverse, in the twinkling of an eye, the world of dust and advance into the realm of holiness; and with one step cover the earth of limitations and reach the domain of the Placeless. It behooveth thee to exert thine utmost to attain unto this Elixir which, in one fleeting breath, causeth the west of ignorance to reach the east of knowledge, illuminates the darkness of night with the resplendence of the morn, guideth the wanderer in the wilderness of doubt to the well-spring of the Divine Presence and Fount of certitude, and conferreth upon mortal souls the honour of acceptance into the Riḍván of immortality.[20]

The source of this amazing power is the Holy Spirit. The term 'Holy Spirit' refers to that spiritual power which is associated with the appearance of the Messengers of God in the world of being. The 'spirit of faith', on the other hand, is the spiritual power which is born in every soul who turns the mirror of the heart towards God and receives the gift of divine knowledge through belief in God's Messenger. It connects the human soul to the Holy Spirit and through that connection brings about the transformation of character.

> All these blessings are brought to man by the Holy Spirit; therefore we can understand that the Holy Spirit is the Intermediary between the Creator and the created. The light and heat of the sun cause the earth to be fruitful, and create life in all things that grow; and the Holy Spirit quickens the souls of men.[21]

> I now assure thee, O servant of God, that, if thy mind become empty and pure from every mention and thought and thy heart attracted wholly to the Kingdom of God, forget all else besides God and come in communion with the Spirit of God, then the Holy Spirit will assist thee with a power which will enable thee to penetrate all things, and a Dazzling Spark which enlightens all sides, a Brilliant Flame in the zenith of the heavens, will teach thee that which thou dost not know of the facts of the universe and of the divine doctrine. Verily, I say unto thee, every soul which ariseth today to guide others to the path of safety and infuse in them the Spirit of Life, the Holy Spirit will inspire that soul with evidences, proofs and facts and the lights will shine upon it from the Kingdom of God.[22]

Bahá'u'lláh in many passages described how those who acquired the spirit of faith during His time performed acts of the greatest courage. He declared:

> And yet, how could they, but for the transformation wrought in their lives, be capable of manifesting such deeds which are contrary to the ways of men and incompatible with their worldly desires?
>
> It is evident that nothing short of this mystic transformation could cause such spirit and behaviour, so utterly unlike their previous habits and manners, to be made manifest in the world of being. For their agitation was turned into peace, their doubt into certitude, their timidity into courage. Such is the potency of the Divine Elixir, which, swift as the twinkling of an eye, transmuteth the souls of men![23]

The influence of love and fear

The following two quotations on the subject of love and fear, appear in Bahá'u'lláh's book *The Four Valleys*:

> Love is a light that never dwelleth in a heart possessed by fear . . . And if he feareth not God, God will make him to fear all things; whereas all things fear him who feareth God.[24]

In this world, without the knowledge of God man is susceptible to every form of fear. For example, if he becomes attached to material wealth, then he will fear losing it; if he does not believe there is life after this life then he will be afraid of death and afraid of losing his loved ones. It is the love of God and understanding of the Word of God which removes fear from the heart. Bahá'u'lláh revealed:

> In the treasuries of the knowledge of God there lieth concealed a knowledge which, when applied, will largely, though not wholly, eliminate fear. This knowledge, however, should be taught from childhood, as it will greatly aid in its elimination. Whatever decreaseth fear increaseth courage.[25]

The love of God and the fear of God are closely related; both have an effect on the transformation of character. The love of God inspires man to express virtues, while the fear of God holds him back from error. When people become afraid of things in this world, that fear is associated with anxiety, weakened willpower and lack of courage, whereas the fear of God is joined to the love of God. They are different facets of the same experience. Both call forth the virtues and inner strength in man; both are factors in his education and the cause of his protection, whereas fear of things in this world incapacitates man.

> From their childhood instil in their hearts the love of God so they may manifest in their lives the fear of God and have confidence in the bestowals of God. Teach them to free themselves from human imperfections and to acquire the divine perfections latent in the heart of man.[26]

One of the strongest moderating influences on man's actions in this world is the knowledge that at the end of this life he will be called to account. This awareness is referred to as the fear of God. The laws governing human society may outwardly regulate man's actions, but fear of God is his inner protection as well.

> . . . that which guardeth and restraineth man both outwardly and inwardly hath been and still is the fear of God. It is man's true protector and his spiritual guardian.[27]

Bahá'u'lláh calls it 'a force that no power can rival',[28] and links it to the protection of mankind.

> The fear of God . . . is the chief cause of the protection of mankind, and the supreme instrument for its preservation. Indeed, there existeth in man a faculty which deterreth him from, and guardeth him against, whatever is unworthy and unseemly, and which is known as his sense of shame. This, however, is confined to but a few; all have not possessed and do not possess it.[29]

CHAPTER 11

THE SOURCE OF HAPPINESS

The more that man understands the powers which influence the soul and the principles that have a bearing on his existence, the clearer the significance of his brief journey through this world will become to him.

The principle that human happiness is founded upon spiritual behaviour

If man's choices in this life are made from his higher nature, and arise from traits such as love, generosity, forgiveness, and patience, he will increase his happiness in this world. If his choices are made on the basis of his material nature and come out of fear, anxiety, anger, impatience, and so on, then he will increase his unhappiness. Situations where choices need to be made come along every day, even many times a day; therefore, the transformation of character and the acquiring of perfections through choosing correctly is a never-ending process and it is a process which begins in childhood.

> In a time to come, morals will degenerate to an extreme degree. It is essential that children be reared in the Bahá'í way, that they may find happiness both in this world and the next. If not, they shall be beset by sorrows and troubles, for human happiness is founded upon spiritual behaviour.[1]

The importance of educating children on the subject of the reality of man cannot be over-stressed; after all, they too are standing in the balance…

> Every child is potentially the light of the world – and at the same time its darkness; wherefore must the question of education be accounted as of primary importance. From his infancy, the child must be nursed at

the breast of God's love, and nurtured in the embrace of His knowledge, that he may radiate light, grow in spirituality, be filled with wisdom and learning, and take on the characteristics of the angelic host.[2]

The importance of action

> The attainment of any object is conditioned upon knowledge, volition and action.[3]

Our physical pilgrimage here would be meaningless if the choices we made in life made no difference at all to our destiny. The very fact that we have the power to choose means that our actions will become the cause of distinguishing ourselves from others.

> Some men and women glory in their exalted thoughts, but if these thoughts never reach the plane of action they remain useless: the power of thought is dependent on its manifestation in deeds.[4]

> Without action nothing in the material world can be accomplished, neither can words unaided advance a man in the spiritual Kingdom.[5]

For those who have been searching for meaning in their lives, the first step taken is the step towards knowledge. When the knowledge of God is attained, and the seeker accepts that God or a supreme creative force exists, and accepts that the divinely inspired Messengers of God appear to train and to educate man, then that seeker must act. With knowledge comes responsibility. The Messenger of God appears to advance the evolution of spiritual man; not only does He prescribe the remedy to correct the ills in human society, but calls on the individual to increasingly express those virtues which are within his higher self.

The gift of guidance

Choosing the spiritual pathway is the greatest bounty and is referred to in the Writings as the 'gift of guidance'.

> By the life of God! verily, the gift of guidance, during this great century and this age of lights, is greater than reigning over the earth and all that

is in it; because the earthly reign is mortal, vanishing, imaginary and of no permanence; but this gift is permanent, eternal, everlasting and endless. Consequently, it is confirmed that this (gift of guidance) is greater than the sovereignty of the world.[6]

Thank God that the evidence and the proof became clear and manifest to thee. He gave thee eyes to see therewith the lights of guidance; He gave thee ears to hear the divine call; He gave thee nostrils to sense the beautiful fragrance of the rose-garden of the Kingdom; He gave thee taste to find the sweetness of the love of God; He gave thee a tongue to mention Him. Therefore, thou must thank Him night and day for having attained this bounty.[7]

Attaining this gift of the knowledge of God is the first step towards transforming character and shifting the focus from this material world to the spiritual world. Another element which can strengthen man's attachment to the spiritual world involves developing a different attitude towards tests and difficulties.

The principle that experiencing tests and difficulties is a bounty

It is hard for man to accept this principle because his material nature is attracted to comfort, safety and ease. Difficulties are endured grudgingly, in spite of the fact that some of the tests encountered are self-inflicted – a consequence of his own actions.

For those who have acquired the spirit of faith, the tests of God can be the cause of progress and spiritual growth.

This spirit of faith is the flame of reality, the life of humanity and the cause of eternal illumination. It inspires man to attain the virtues and perfections of the divine world.[8]

However, in the absence of the spiritual strength which comes from the knowledge of God and the love of God, tests may have quite the opposite effect.

... the divine trials cause some souls to become entirely lifeless, while they cause the holy souls to ascend to the highest degree of love and solidity. They cause progress and they also cause retrogression.[9]

To the loyal soul, a test is but God's grace and favour; for the valiant doth joyously press forward to furious battle on the field of anguish, when the coward, whimpering with fright, will tremble and shake. So too, the proficient student, who hath with great competence mastered his subjects and committed them to memory, will happily exhibit his skills before his examiners on the day of his tests. So too will solid gold wondrously gleam and shine out in the assayer's fire.

It is clear, then, that tests and trials are, for sanctified souls, but God's bounty and grace, while to the weak, they are a calamity, unexpected and sudden.[10]

The principle of separation and distinction

The nature of life in this world and man's spiritual growth is governed by something which Bahá'u'lláh called the 'principle of separation and distinction'.[11]

The mere fact that such a principle exists conveys the message that life is not always going to be easy. 'Testing' is part of the divine purpose; it provides the means whereby 'the pure in spirit and the detached in heart . . . they who seek the Beauty of the All-Glorious may be distinguished and separated from the wayward and perverse.'[12] This principle is also referred to by Muhammad in the Qur'án (29:2, quoted here by Bahá'u'lláh):

> Even as He hath revealed: 'Do men think when they say "We believe" they shall be let alone and not be put to proof?'[13]

When man faces and overcomes tests and difficulties, this has a powerful and positive influence on the development of the soul in this world. For example, as stated before, man may be tested by material things; his attachment to them (or detachment from them) becomes the means by which his worthiness is proved. This is one of many ways that the principle of separation and distinction operates.

The subject of suffering in this world

The following passages are a selection from the many references made by 'Abdu'l-Bahá to the subject of suffering:

> The mind and spirit of man advance when he is tried by suffering. The more the ground is ploughed the better the seed will grow, the better the harvest will be. Just as the plough furrows the earth deeply, purifying it of weeds and thistles, so suffering and tribulation free man from the petty affairs of this worldly life until he arrives at a state of complete detachment. His attitude in this world will be that of divine happiness. Man is, so to speak, unripe: the heat of the fire of suffering will mature him. Look back to the times past and you will find that the greatest men have suffered most . . .
>
> To attain eternal happiness one must suffer. He who has reached the state of self-sacrifice has true joy. Temporal joy will vanish.[14]

> Men who suffer not, attain no perfection. The plant most pruned by the gardeners is that one which, when the summer comes, will have the most beautiful blossoms and the most abundant fruit.[15]

> Those who suffer most, attain to the greatest perfection.[16]

It may be hard to accept that any form of personal distress or misery could be beneficial in any way – particularly for those in the middle of such experiences, which is why this fact is often not appreciated until much later. Certainly, those who believe in this principle will find it easier to accept that enduring suffering and experiencing hardship can be a positive force in life.

> Physical pain is a necessary accompaniment of all human existence, and as such is unavoidable. As long as there will be life on earth, there will be also suffering, in various forms and degrees. But suffering, although an inescapable reality, can nevertheless be utilized as a means for the attainment of happiness . . . In every suffering one can find a meaning and a wisdom. But it is not always easy to find the secret of that wisdom. It is sometimes only when all our suffering has passed that we become aware of its usefulness. What man considers to be evil

turns often to be a cause of infinite blessings. And this is due to his desire to know more than he can. God's wisdom is, indeed, inscrutable to us all, and it is no use pushing too far trying to discover that which shall always remain a mystery to our mind.[17]

The mystery of sacrifice

That is to say, man must sacrifice the qualities and attributes of the world of nature for the qualities and attributes of the world of God. For instance, consider the substance we call iron. Observe its qualities; it is solid, black, cold. These are the characteristics of iron. When the same iron absorbs heat from the fire, it sacrifices its attribute of solidity for the attribute of fluidity. It sacrifices its attribute of darkness for the attribute of light, which is a quality of the fire. It sacrifices its attribute of coldness to the quality of heat which the fire possesses so that in the iron there remains no solidity, darkness or cold. It becomes illumined and transformed, having sacrificed its qualities to the qualities and attributes of the fire . . .

Every man trained through the teachings of God and illumined by the light of His guidance, who becomes a believer in God and His signs and is enkindled with the fire of the love of God, sacrifices the imperfections of nature for the sake of divine perfections. Consequently, every perfect person, every illumined, heavenly individual stands in the station of sacrifice.[18]

The lover and the watchman

The story of the lover and the watchman in Bahá'u'lláh's mystical work *The Seven Valleys* illustrates the principle of the hidden reward in suffering:

There was once a lover who had sighed for long years in separation from his beloved, and wasted in the fire of remoteness. From the rule of love, his heart was empty of patience, and his body weary of his spirit; he reckoned life without her as a mockery, and time consumed him away. How many a day he found no rest in longing for her; how many a night the pain of her kept him from sleep; his body was worn to a sigh, his heart's wound had turned him to a cry of sorrow. He had given a thousand lives for one taste of the cup of her presence, but it availed him not. The doctors knew no cure for him, and companions avoided his company; yea, physicians have no medicine for one sick of love, unless the favour of the beloved one deliver him.

At last, the tree of his longing yielded the fruit of despair, and the fire of his hope fell to ashes. Then one night he could live no more, and he went out of his house and made for the marketplace. On a sudden, a watchman followed after him. He broke into a run, with the watchman following; then other watchmen came together, and barred every passage to the weary one. And the wretched one cried from his heart, and ran here and there, and moaned to himself: 'Surely this watchman is Izrá'íl, my angel of death, following so fast upon me; or he is a tyrant of men, seeking to harm me.' His feet carried him on, the one bleeding with the arrow of love, and his heart lamented. Then he came to a garden wall, and with untold pain he scaled it, for it proved very high; and forgetting his life, he threw himself down to the garden.

And there he beheld his beloved with a lamp in her hand, searching for a ring she had lost. When the heart-surrendered lover looked on his ravishing love, he drew a great breath and raised up his hands in prayer, crying: 'O God! Give Thou glory to the watchman, and riches and long life. For the watchman was Gabriel, guiding this poor one; or he was Isráfíl, bringing life to this wretched one!'

Indeed, his words were true, for he had found many a secret justice in this seeming tyranny of the watchman, and seen how many a mercy lay hid behind the veil. Out of wrath, the guard had led him who was athirst in love's desert to the sea of his loved one, and lit up the dark night of absence with the light of reunion. He had driven one who was afar, into the garden of nearness, had guided an ailing soul to the heart's physician.

Now if the lover could have looked ahead, he would have blessed the watchman at the start, and prayed on his behalf, and he would have seen that tyranny as justice; but since the end was veiled to him, he moaned and made his plaint in the beginning. Yet those who journey in the garden-land of knowledge, because they see the end in the beginning, see peace in war and friendliness in anger.[19]

Joy and pain

In the following transcript of a talk given by 'Abdu'l-Bahá in 1911, He affirms that the life of every person is touched by the influences of joy and pain, but that when our thoughts are anchored in the spiritual kingdom, we are better able to cope with 'material anxiety'.

In this world we are influenced by two sentiments, *Joy* and *Pain*.

Joy gives us wings! In times of joy our strength is more vital, our intellect keener, and our understanding less clouded. We seem better able to cope with the world and to find our sphere of usefulness. But when sadness visits us we become weak, our strength leaves us, our comprehension is dim and our intelligence veiled. The actualities of life seem to elude our grasp, the eyes of our spirits fail to discover the sacred mysteries, and we become even as dead beings.

There is no human being untouched by these two influences; but all the sorrow and the grief that exist come from the world of matter – the spiritual world bestows only the joy!

If we suffer it is the outcome of material things, and all the trials and troubles come from this world of illusion.

For instance, a merchant may lose his trade and depression ensues. A workman is dismissed and starvation stares him in the face. A farmer has a bad harvest, anxiety fills his mind. A man builds a house which is burnt to the ground and he is straightway homeless, ruined, and in despair.

All these examples are to show you that the trials which beset our every step, all our sorrow, pain, shame and grief, are born in the world of matter; whereas the spiritual Kingdom never causes sadness. A man living with his thoughts in this Kingdom knows perpetual joy. The ills all flesh is heir to do not pass him by, but they only touch the surface of his life, the depths are calm and serene.

Today, humanity is bowed down with trouble, sorrow and grief, no one escapes; the world is wet with tears; but, thank God, the remedy is at our doors. Let us turn our hearts away from the world of matter and live in the spiritual world! It alone can give us freedom! If we are hemmed in by difficulties we have only to call upon God, and by His great Mercy we shall be helped.

If sorrow and adversity visit us, let us turn our faces to the Kingdom and heavenly consolation will be outpoured.

If we are sick and in distress let us implore God's healing, and He will answer our prayer.

When our thoughts are filled with the bitterness of this world, let us turn our eyes to the sweetness of God's compassion and He will send us heavenly calm! If we are imprisoned in the material world, our spirit can soar into the Heavens and we shall be free indeed!

When our days are drawing to a close let us think of the eternal worlds, and we shall be full of joy!

You see all round you proofs of the inadequacy of material things – how joy, comfort, peace and consolation are not to be found in the transitory things of the world. Is it not then foolishness to refuse to seek these treasures where they may be found? The doors of the spiritual Kingdom are open to all, and without is absolute darkness.

Thank God that you in this assembly have this knowledge, for in all the sorrows of life you can obtain supreme consolation. If your days on earth are numbered, you know that everlasting life awaits you. If material anxiety envelops you in a dark cloud, spiritual radiance lightens your path. Verily, those whose minds are illumined by the Spirit of the Most High have supreme consolation.[20]

The principle that life was created for happiness

As to spiritual happiness, this is the true basis of the life of man, for life was created for happiness, not for sorrow; for pleasure, not for grief. Happiness is life; sorrow is death. Spiritual happiness is life eternal . . .

Were it not for this happiness the world of existence would not have been created.[21]

Making sacrifices and experiencing sadness from time to time are aspects of life that are inescapable, but these things do not necessarily need to result in unhappiness. This physical life may be fleeting, but life was created for happiness, and in this world true happiness comes from our higher nature; it is a spiritual happiness associated with the love of God. It is not the same as the happiness which derives from having material comfort.

The true test of nobility lies in being able to remain happy throughout life in spite of what we have to face.

Anybody can be happy in the state of comfort, ease, health, success, pleasure and joy; but if one will be happy and contented in the time of trouble, hardship and prevailing disease, it is the proof of nobility.[22]

At all times, the key to this happiness is the remembrance of God.

> If thy daily living become difficult, soon (God) thy Lord will bestow upon thee that which shall satisfy thee. Be patient in the time of affliction and trial, endure every difficulty and hardship with a dilated heart, attracted spirit and eloquent tongue in remembrance of the Merciful. Verily this is the life of satisfaction, the spiritual existence, heavenly repose, divine benediction and the celestial table! Soon thy Lord will extenuate thy straitened circumstances even in this world.[23]

> The honour of man is through the attainment of the knowledge of God; his happiness is from the love of God; his joy is in the glad tidings of God; his greatness is dependent upon his servitude to God.[24]

The principle that life is a process

> Life is a process of trials and testings, and these are – contrary to what we are prone to thinking – good for us, and give us stamina, and teach us to rely on God.[25]

Some religious communities place a great deal of emphasis on events – for example, much Christian theology focuses on 'the Crucifixion', 'the Resurrection', and 'the Second Coming' or 'Rapture' (an event during which many Christians believe that Christ will descend from the physical clouds and the faithful souls will rise up to meet him in the air). People have a tendency to focus on specific events, rather than seeing the whole picture, yet the reality in both the spiritual and material sense is that all things are involved in one process or another. Note these examples taken from the Writings:

Creation:

> The process of His creation hath had no beginning, and can have no end.[26]

Virtues:

> ... the virtues of the human world are in the process of unfoldment.[27]

Cellular elements:

> Their journeyings through material phenomena are continuous. Therefore, each phenomenon is the expression in degree of all other phenomena. The difference is one of successive transferences and the period of time involved in evolutionary process.[28]

The appearance of the Messengers of God:

> The process of the rise and setting of the Sun of Truth will thus indefinitely continue – a process that hath had no beginning and will have no end.[29]

Even the outpouring of knowledge associated with the appearance of the divine Messenger is a gradual process – necessarily, as a mercy to mankind.

> . . . in every Dispensation the light of Divine Revelation hath been vouchsafed unto men in direct proportion to their spiritual capacity. Consider the sun. How feeble its rays the moment it appeareth above the horizon. How gradually its warmth and potency increase as it approacheth its zenith, enabling meanwhile all created things to adapt themselves to the growing intensity of its light. How steadily it declineth until it reacheth its setting point. Were it, all of a sudden, to manifest the energies latent within it, it would, no doubt, cause injury to all created things . . . In like manner, if the Sun of Truth were suddenly to reveal, at the earliest stages of its manifestation, the full measure of the potencies which the providence of the Almighty hath bestowed upon it, the earth of human understanding would waste away and be consumed; for men's hearts would neither sustain the intensity of its revelation, nor be able to mirror forth the radiance of its light.[30]

Once it is accepted that life is a 'process', it is possible to look at the 'events' in life in a different way. The expectation that significant changes will come about in life once certain events have happened can lead to disappointment. Changes come about when someone decides to do things differently from what he or she has been doing and then acts on those decisions. It is an internal process having to do with the mind and thought, not with external events.

> The reality of man is his thought, not his material body.[31]

The same truth is stated in the Old Testament: 'For as he thinketh in his heart, so is he.'[32]

Events do not always fulfil the expectations that people have of them, and religious history certainly reflects this observation. For example, the appearance of Christ and the declaration of His mission in the midst of that community was a major event; yet, because He did not fulfil certain prophecies of the Torah in the style and in the manner that the Jews expected, they rejected Him.

> Two thousand years ago the Israelites expected the Messiah. Day and night they were praying in the temple, supplicating in the holy of holies, crying, 'O God, send to us the true one, our deliverer and redeemer' – thus they lamented and bemoaned his delay. But when His Holiness the Christ appeared they jeeringly turned away; when the orb of reality dawned they could not see it, for their eyes were covered with the veils of traditions and names. These anxious waiting ones did not become the recipients of that bestowal; nor hearken to the call of God; nor quaff from the chalice of love; nor behold the rays of the sun of reality. It is now nearly two thousand years since their Messiah appeared and still they await him![33]

The Christian world likewise failed to recognize the dawning of Muhammad's Revelation. This highlights the truth that, when tested, members of established religious communities tend to cling to the 'lamp' and disregard the renewal and appearance of the light.

The principle of leaving the important for the most important

How many people hope that their lives will change for the better when certain events take place? For example,

'When I turn 18 . . .' 'When I leave home . . .' 'When I get a job . . .' 'When I've completed my degree . . .' 'When I've made enough money . . .' 'When I get married . . .' 'When the children have left home . . .' 'When I retire . . .'

But things do not always go smoothly or according to plan; unforeseen problems arise that lead to decisions being deferred or actions being delayed. For some people the result is that they do not use their capacities to the full, and, as time passes, find that they have arrived at 'check-out' earlier than they expected to, not having done many of the things they really wanted to do.

The greatest achievements of one's life may well be accomplished during the most difficult and trying periods; to wait until conditions are perfect may result in missed opportunities. If it is a very important matter, don't wait!

> . . . we must sacrifice the important for the most important.[34]

Remaining calm in the storm

> . . . the loving believers also accept and remain submissive to God's Will, content with it, radiantly acquiescent, offering thanks.[35]

Those who believe in processes come to accept tests and difficulties as a necessary element in their growth and development and *know* that life is unlikely to ever settle down. Along with the rest of the human race they cannot avoid these things, yet they are able to remain contented in spite of them by maintaining a spiritual focus throughout their lives.

> A man living with his thoughts in this Kingdom knows perpetual joy. The ills all flesh is heir to do not pass him by, but they only touch the surface of his life, the depths are calm and serene.[36]

The principle of uncertainty

There are few things in life that man can be certain of; the truth is that life in this world is uncertain. Real safety and true security can be found only under God's protection.

> Man must seek shelter in the mercy and protection of God, for he is constantly subject to a hundred thousand dangers. Save for the refuge and protection of the Most High, man is without shelter.[37]

> I swear by Thy might! No refuge is there to flee to except Thee, and

no shelter to seek except Thy shelter, and no protection except Thy protection.[38]

There is no retreat nor way of flight for anyone save unto God, and no refuge nor asylum but in Him.[39]

When man accepts the existence of God and His Messengers he will begin to appreciate that everything happening in this world has some spiritual significance, and when he puts his trust in God, then he will no longer be fearful or concerned about the uncertainties associated with life in this world.

Trusting in God

Be not afraid of anyone, place thy whole trust in God, the Almighty, the All-Knowing.[40]

I implore Thee, O Thou that turnest darkness into light, and revealest Thy mysteries on the Sinai of Thy Revelation, to aid me, at all times, to put my trust in Thee, and to commit mine affairs unto Thy care. Make me, then, O my God, content with that which the finger of Thy decree hath traced, and the pen of Thy ordinance hath written. Potent art Thou to do what pleaseth Thee, and in Thy grasp are the reins of all that are in heaven and on earth.[41]

He that giveth up himself wholly to God, God shall, assuredly, be with him; and he that placeth his complete trust in God, God shall, verily, protect him from whatsoever may harm him, and shield him from the wickedness of every evil plotter.[42]

Cause me, then, to turn wholly unto Thee, to put my whole trust in Thee, to seek Thee as my Refuge, and to flee unto Thy face. Thou art, verily, He Who, through the power of His might, doeth whatsoever He desireth, and commandeth, through the potency of His will, whatsoever He chooseth.[43]

You should . . . leave all your affairs in His Hands, place your trust in Him, and rely upon Him. He will assuredly not forsake you. In this, likewise, there is no doubt. No father will surrender his sons to devouring beasts; no shepherd will leave his flock to ravening wolves.[44]

If the heart turns away from the blessings God offers how can it hope for happiness? If it does not put its hope and trust in God's Mercy, where can it find rest? Oh, trust in God! for His Bounty is everlasting, and in His Blessings, for they are superb. Oh! put your faith in the Almighty, for He faileth not and His goodness endureth for ever! His Sun giveth Light continually, and the Clouds of His Mercy are full of the Waters of Compassion with which He waters the hearts of all who trust in Him. His refreshing Breeze ever carries healing in its wings to the parched souls of men! Is it wise to turn away from such a loving Father, Who showers His blessings upon us, and to choose rather to be slaves of matter?[45]

Trust in the favour of God. Look not at your own capacities, for the divine bestowal can transform a drop into an ocean; it can make a tiny seed a lofty tree.[46]

Rely upon God. Trust in Him. Praise Him, and call Him continually to mind. He verily turneth trouble into ease, and sorrow into solace, and toil into utter peace. He verily hath dominion over all things.[47]

A Prayer

O Lord! Unto Thee I repair for refuge and toward all Thy signs I set my heart.
 O Lord! Whether travelling or at home, and in my occupation or in my work, I place my whole trust in Thee.
 Grant me then Thy sufficing help so as to make me independent of all things, O Thou Who art unsurpassed in Thy mercy! . . .
 Thine is the absolute authority to command.[48]

CHAPTER 12

DEPARTING THIS LIFE

In the previous chapters, the purpose of this life has been linked to the understanding of our true reality, our divine nature, and to the development of spiritual attributes, which have to varying degrees been deposited within every human being.

The acceptance that our true nature is spiritual makes it possible to see everything that happens during this life in a new light and to understand that death is nothing to be afraid of. The purpose of life in this world is to prepare ourselves for the next world. It is for this reason that the Messengers of God appear.

> The purpose underlying their revelation hath been to educate all men, that they may, at the hour of death, ascend, in the utmost purity and sanctity and with absolute detachment, to the throne of the Most High.[1]

Painful experiences and suffering are the lot of every person, but those who understand their spiritual basis can use these things to strengthen the spiritual faculties, increasing those powers that can be exercised in the spiritual worlds of God.

Preparing for the next world

The embryo in the mother's womb is destined to automatically develop those physical parts necessary to life in this existence: eyes, ears, limbs and so on – in spite of the fact that it has no need of them before the moment of birth. In the matrix of this world the human soul is also developing, but unlike the growth of the foetus, the realization of *spiritual attributes* so necessary for life in the next world is not automatic. This development is entirely our own responsibility. These attributes are acquired through man's free will, through his own volition.

> Therefore, in this world he must prepare himself for the life beyond. That which he needs in the world of the Kingdom must be obtained here. Just as he prepared himself in the world of the matrix by acquiring forces necessary in this sphere of existence, so, likewise, the indispensable forces of the divine existence must be potentially attained in this world.
>
> What is he in need of in the Kingdom which transcends the life and limitation of this mortal sphere? That world beyond is a world of sanctity and radiance; therefore, it is necessary that in this world he should acquire these divine attributes. In that world there is need of spirituality, faith, assurance, the knowledge and love of God. These he must attain in this world so that after his ascension from the earthly to the heavenly Kingdom he shall find all that is needful in that eternal life ready for him.
>
> That divine world is manifestly a world of lights; therefore, man has need of illumination here. That is a world of love; the love of God is essential. It is a world of perfections; virtues, or perfections, must be acquired. That world is vivified by the breaths of the Holy Spirit; in this world we must seek them. That is the Kingdom of everlasting life; it must be attained during this vanishing existence.
>
> By what means can man acquire these things? How shall he obtain these merciful gifts and powers? First, through the knowledge of God. Second, through the love of God. Third, through faith. Fourth, through philanthropic deeds. Fifth, through self-sacrifice. Sixth, through severance from this world. Seventh, through sanctity and holiness.[2]

This world and the next world co-exist

The unborn child within the womb of its mother cannot have any idea of the world it is soon to be born into and yet that world is astonishingly close to it, hidden only by a thin veil, the abdominal wall of its mother. At present we are within the womb of this material world, moving towards and preparing ourselves for that moment when we will be born (at the moment of death) into the spiritual world. The veil between this world and the next is also very thin and, just like the baby, we are unable to penetrate that veil – the next world is completely hidden.

This simple analogy of the child existing in two worlds at the same time demonstrates that the spiritual world is not something awaiting, pending, or in the future; it exists – here – now. If the spiritual worlds of God did not exist, the appearance of the human reality in this world would be pointless. The birth of the child into this world illustrates this truth and provides an undeniable argument for the existence of the next world.

Another observation that can be made about the example of the unborn child is that this world surrounds the world of the womb. If we now consider this world and the next world, the same principle can be applied, that is, the spiritual world surrounds this world. Adib Taherzadeh explains this:

> One of the principles of nature is that higher forms of life revolve around, and depend upon, the lowest. In this physical world we observe that all living things derive their sustenance from the mineral world, which is the lower kingdom. This earth, although the lowest form of life, gives birth to higher forms and may be regarded as a pivot round which the kingdoms of the vegetable, the animal and man revolve. Similarly, the spiritual worlds of God, as testified by Bahá'u'lláh in His Tablets, revolve around this world, the world of man. This means that the next world is not divorced from life in this world, but rather encompasses it.[3]

That is also how 'Abdu'l-Bahá described the human spirit; He called it 'an all-encompassing power' and 'a circumambient power that encompasseth the realities of all things'.[4]

The world of existence is a single world

Words such as 'inner', 'innermost' and 'within' are also used to allude to the spiritual world, and these words convey a sense of the connection between this world and the next.

The fact that the different worlds of God exist alongside each other is confirmed by 'Abdu'l-Bahá.

> . . . know ye that the world of existence is a single world, although its stations are various and distinct.[5]

> Those souls who are pure and unsullied, upon the dissolution of their elemental frames, hasten away to the world of God, and that world is within this world. The people of this world, however, are unaware of that world, and are even as the mineral and the vegetable that know nothing of the world of the animal and the world of man.[6]

Our friends and loved ones who have departed this life have not gone away entirely; they have simply shed the 'physical garment' and entered a world which cannot be seen but which exists alongside this world. The world of existence is a single world; the spiritual realm that they have entered surrounds this world and they continue to exist; therefore, they are in a sense near to us.

> Those who have ascended have different attributes from those who are still on earth, yet there is no real separation.[7]

The mystery of the connection between souls that have left this world and souls that remain here has never been fully revealed, but prayer is the channel through which a mutual intercession can take place. The progress of a departed soul can be affected by the prayers of people in this world and, mysteriously, souls in the next world can also intercede for those that remain here in this life.*

Meditating on the next world

Clearly there is a great difference between what is called physical and what is called spiritual, yet the Writings state that they are intimately connected, that the outward physical world is a reflection of the inner world of the spirit:

> The worlds of God are in perfect harmony and correspondence one with another. Each world in this limitless universe is, as it were, a mirror reflecting the history and nature of all the rest. The physical universe is, likewise, in perfect correspondence with the spiritual or divine realm. The world of matter is an outer expression or facsimile of

---

* This connection is different from that claimed by spiritualists who assert that people can make contact with those who have passed on, or receive messages via a medium.

the inner kingdom of spirit. The world of minds corresponds with the world of hearts.[8]

The law of attraction, the 'power of love', is the cause of the existence of the whole phenomenal universe, and the way in which the human soul is attracted to the next world is an expression of that same spiritual law. Man 'knows' through the heavenly intellectual power that the next world exists, and as the powers of the soul develop through acquiring divine attributes, so also does the intensity of attraction between the soul and the next world increase.

In the early days of the birth of a new Revelation from God, those fortunate enough to come into direct contact with the Messenger of God became so transformed and transfigured by their love of God that they yearned for the next world. That transforming power, evident in the persons of the Messengers of God, is also invested in Their revealed words. In every Revelation it is the Word of God which provides the blueprint for right action and spiritual growth. Studying and meditating on that Word is the door to the knowledge and love of God. 'Abdu'l-Bahá referred to the need for man to acquire a thirst for spirituality and further declared that 'the way to acquire this thirst is to meditate upon the future life.'[9]

> Life is a load which must be carried on while we are on earth, but the cares of the lower things of life should not be allowed to monopolize all the thoughts and aspirations of a human being. The heart's ambitions should ascend to a more glorious goal, mental activity should rise to higher levels! Men should hold in their souls the vision of celestial perfection, and there prepare a dwelling-place for the inexhaustible bounty of the Divine Spirit.[10]

> The meditative faculty is akin to the mirror; if you put it before earthly objects it will reflect them. Therefore if the spirit of man is contemplating earthly subjects he will be informed of these.
>
> But if you turn the mirror of your spirits heavenwards, the heavenly constellations and the rays of the Sun of Reality will be reflected in your hearts, and the virtues of the Kingdom will be obtained.[11]

The moment of physical death

> Our body is like the cage, and the spirit is like the bird. We see that without the cage this bird flies... therefore, if the cage becomes broken, the bird will continue and exist. Its feelings will be even more powerful, its perceptions greater, and its happiness increased.[12]

At the moment of physical death the soul leaves the body, much like a caged bird escaping from its enclosure; it is born into a new and limitless existence beyond the restrictions of this physical world. It seems to those remaining in this world that death has completely cut off their loved ones, yet the soul after its separation from the body continues to be aware of this world.

'Abdu'l-Bahá explains that at that moment when the soul is born into the next world, the veil 'interposed' by God between that world and this will be lifted away and it will become aware of the next world; previously hidden matters, including knowledge of the spiritual station of other souls, will be revealed to that soul.

> When the human soul soareth out of this transient heap of dust and riseth into the world of God, then veils will fall away, and verities will come to light, and all things unknown before will be made clear, and hidden truths be understood.[13]

> As to thy question regarding discoveries made by the soul after it hath put off its human form: certainly, that world is a world of perceptions and discoveries, for the interposed veil will be lifted away and the human spirit will gaze upon souls that are above, below, and on a par with itself.[14]

We are counselled to show the greatest respect for the body of someone who has died, treating it as if the soul were still present. This honouring of 'the throne of the inner temple' acknowledges the unique relationship between the soul and the body in this world.

> As this physical frame is the throne of the inner temple, whatever occurs to the former is felt by the latter. In reality that which takes delight in joy or is saddened by pain is the inner temple of the body, not the

body itself. Since this physical body is the throne whereon the inner temple is established, God hath ordained that the body be preserved to the extent possible, so that nothing that causeth repugnance may be experienced. The inner temple beholdeth its physical frame, which is its throne. Thus, if the latter is accorded respect, it is as if the former is the recipient. The converse is likewise true.

Therefore, it hath been ordained that the dead body should be treated with the utmost honour and respect.[15]

As it is beyond man's capacity to understand the next world, descriptions of life hereafter are not to be found in the Writings; rather, there are statements such as these:

The world beyond is as different from this world as this world is different from that of the child while still in the womb of its mother.[16]

... the Kingdom is not a material place; it is sanctified from time and place. It is a spiritual world, a divine world, and the centre of the Sovereignty of God; it is freed from body and that which is corporeal, and it is purified and sanctified from the imaginations of the human world. To be limited to place is a property of bodies and not of spirits. Place and time surround the body, not the mind and spirit.[17]

The moment of realization

When born into the spiritual world, the outcome of our journey through this world will be realized – all our actions here will stand revealed there. In short, we shall evaluate our lives.

It is clear and evident that all men shall, after their physical death, estimate the worth of their deeds, and realize all that their hands have wrought.[18]

For just as the effects and the fruitage of the uterine life are not to be found in that dark and narrow place, and only when the child is transferred to this wide earth do the benefits and uses of growth and development in that previous world become revealed – so likewise reward and punishment, heaven and hell, requital and retribution for actions done in this present life, will stand revealed in that other world beyond. And just as, if human life in the womb were limited to that uterine world, existence there would be nonsensical, irrelevant – so too if the life of this world, the deeds here done and their fruitage, did not come forth in the world beyond, the whole process would be irrational and foolish.[19]

Entering the realm of light

Although the next world is not visible, there are several passages in the Writings that help us to accept its reality and presence. For example, 'Abdu'l-Bahá in the following moving passages uses the analogy of the child in the womb, which He says 'expresses the relation of the temporal world to the life hereafter'. This talk was given on 23 April 1912 in Washington, DC, in order to comfort the hearts of those people who were deeply saddened upon hearing news of the *Titanic* disaster.

> These human conditions may be likened to the matrix of the mother from which a child is to be born into the spacious outer world. At first the infant finds it very difficult to reconcile itself to its new existence. It cries as if not wishing to be separated from its narrow abode and imagining that life is restricted to that limited space. It is reluctant to leave its home, but nature forces it into this world. Having come into its new conditions, it finds that it has passed from darkness into a sphere of radiance; from gloomy and restricted surroundings it has been transferred to a spacious and delightful environment. Its nourishment was the blood of the mother; now it finds delicious food to enjoy. Its new life is filled with brightness and beauty; it looks with wonder and delight upon the mountains, meadows and fields of green, the rivers and fountains, the wonderful stars; it breathes the life-quickening atmosphere; and then it praises God for its release from the confinement of its former condition and attainment to the freedom of a new realm. This analogy expresses the relation of the temporal world to the life hereafter – the transition of the soul of man from darkness and uncertainty to the light and reality of the eternal Kingdom. At first it is very difficult to welcome death, but after attaining its new condition the soul is grateful, for it has been released from the bondage of the limited to enjoy the liberties of the unlimited. It has been freed from a world of sorrow, grief and trials to live in a world of unending bliss and

joy. The phenomenal and physical have been abandoned in order that it may attain the opportunities of the ideal and spiritual. Therefore, the souls of those who have passed away from earth and completed their span of mortal pilgrimage in the *Titanic* disaster have hastened to a world superior to this. They have soared away from these conditions of darkness and dim vision into the realm of light. These are the only considerations which can comfort and console those whom they have left behind.

Furthermore, these events have deeper reasons. Their object and purpose is to teach man certain lessons. We are living in a day of reliance upon material conditions. Men imagine that the great size and strength of a ship, the perfection of machinery or the skill of a navigator will ensure safety, but these disasters sometimes take place that men may know that God is the real Protector. If it be the will of God to protect man, a little ship may escape destruction, whereas the greatest and most perfectly constructed vessel with the best and most skilful navigator may not survive a danger such as was present on the ocean. The purpose is that the people of the world may turn to God, the One Protector; that human souls may rely upon His preservation and know that He is the real safety. These events happen in order that man's faith may be increased and strengthened. Therefore, although we feel sad and disheartened, we must supplicate God to turn our hearts to the Kingdom and pray for these departed souls with faith in His infinite mercy so that, although they have been deprived of this earthly life, they may enjoy a new existence in the supreme mansions of the Heavenly Father.

Let no one imagine that these words imply that man should not be thorough and careful in his undertakings. God has endowed man with intelligence so that he may safeguard and protect himself. Therefore, he must provide and surround himself with all that scientific skill can produce. He must be deliberate, thoughtful and thorough in his purposes, build the best ship and provide the most experienced captain; yet, withal, let him rely upon God and consider God as the one Keeper. If God protects, nothing can imperil man's safety; and if it be not His will to safeguard, no amount of preparation and precaution will avail.[20]

In this world, separation is inevitable

The bond of love between people can be very strong and, when broken by death, a deep sadness is experienced. Being no longer able to touch, hold, embrace them or talk with them makes this separation very painful and, at times, the sense of loss can be almost unbearable. As separation through death is inevitable, 'Abdu'l-Bahá explains that man cannot escape these strong emotions. During His life He wrote many prayers and Tablets to comfort people who were bereaved. For example, the following beautiful Tablet was revealed for a mother who had lost a son:

> O thou beloved maid-servant of God, although the loss of a son is indeed heart-breaking and beyond the limits of human endurance, yet one who knoweth and understandeth is assured that the son hath not been lost but, rather, hath stepped from this world into another, and she will find him in the divine realm. That reunion shall be for eternity, while in this world separation is inevitable and bringeth with it a burning grief.
>
> Praise be unto God that thou hast faith, art turning thy face toward the everlasting Kingdom and believest in the existence of a heavenly world. Therefore be thou not disconsolate, do not languish, do not sigh, neither wail nor weep; for agitation and mourning deeply affect his soul in the divine realm.
>
> That beloved child addresseth thee from the hidden world: 'O thou kind Mother, thank divine Providence that I have been freed from a small and gloomy cage and, like the birds of the meadows, have soared to the divine world – a world which is spacious, illumined, and ever gay and jubilant. Therefore, lament not, O Mother, and be not grieved; I am not of the lost, nor have I been obliterated and destroyed. I have shaken off the mortal form and have raised my banner in this spiritual world. Following this separation is everlasting companionship. Thou shalt find me in the heaven of the Lord, immersed in an ocean of light.'[21]

And in another Tablet are these words of consolation:

> The inscrutable divine wisdom underlies such heart-rending occurrences. It is as if a kind gardener transferreth a fresh and tender shrub from a confined place to a wide open area. This transfer is not the

cause of the withering, the lessening or the destruction of that shrub; nay, on the contrary, it maketh it to grow and thrive, acquire freshness and delicacy, become green and bear fruit. This hidden secret is well known to the gardener, but those souls who are unaware of this bounty suppose that the gardener, in his anger and wrath, hath uprooted the shrub. Yet to those who are aware, this concealed fact is manifest and this predestined decree is considered a bounty. Do not feel grieved or disconsolate, therefore, at the ascension of that bird of faithfulness; nay, under all circumstances pray for that youth, supplicating for him forgiveness and the elevation of his station.[22]

Praying for the departed

The importance of praying for those who have gone to the next world cannot be overstated. Prayer is the means by which spiritual bonds are created, and praying for others in the next world is much like establishing a wonderful lasting friendship and affinity with someone in this life; just as people are able to support and assist each other here in this world, prayer provides the means to accomplish the same thing in a spiritual sense between this world and the next. The following is one of many prayers for the departed contained in the Bahá'í Writings:

> O my God! O Thou forgiver of sins, bestower of gifts, dispeller of afflictions!
> Verily, I beseech Thee to forgive the sins of such as have abandoned the physical garment and have ascended to the spiritual world.
> O my Lord! Purify them from trespasses, dispel their sorrows, and change their darkness into light. Cause them to enter the garden of happiness, cleanse them with the most pure water, and grant them to behold Thy splendours on the loftiest mount.[23]

While he remains in this world man has absolute control over his own spiritual progress.

For the faith of no man can be conditioned by any one except himself.[24]

But once having passed from this world, the progress of the soul is according to the bounty of God and also through the intercession of others.

Those still in this world can choose to assist those who have passed beyond the realm of choice. Although our loved ones may have left their physical bodies behind and entered the spiritual world, it is still possible to love them, to pray for them and to perform acts of charity in their name to assist them there. This is our great privilege.

> The progress of man's spirit in the divine world, after the severance of its connection with the body of dust, is through the bounty and grace of the Lord alone, or through the intercession and the sincere prayers of other human souls, or through the charities and important good works which are performed in its name.[25]

> As the spirit of man after putting off this material form has an everlasting life, certainly any existing being is capable of making progress; therefore it is permitted to ask for advancement, forgiveness, mercy, beneficence, and blessings for a man after his death, because existence is capable of progression. That is why in the prayers of Bahá'u'lláh forgiveness and remission of sins are asked for those who have died. Moreover, as people in this world are in need of God, they will also need Him in the other world. The creatures are always in need, and God is absolutely independent, whether in this world or in the world to come.[26]

This knowledge, that those who have passed on can be assisted through our prayers and through our actions in this world, provides the means to channel our sadness and grief in the most positive way. 'Abdu'l-Bahá encourages us to do this, especially for our parents.

> Also a father and mother endure the greatest troubles and hardships for their children; and often when the children have reached the age of maturity, the parents pass on to the other world. Rarely does it happen that a father and mother in this world see the reward of the care and trouble they have undergone for their children. Therefore, children, in return for this care and trouble, must show forth charity and beneficence, and must implore pardon and forgiveness for their parents.[27]

The same power in the other world

> As we have power to pray for these souls here, so likewise we shall possess the same power in the other world, which is the Kingdom of God. Are not all the people in that world the creatures of God? Therefore, in that world also they can make progress. As here they can receive light by their supplication, there also they can plead for forgiveness, and receive light through entreaties and supplications. Thus as souls in this world, through the help of the supplications, the entreaties, and the prayers of the holy ones, can acquire development, so is it the same after death. Through their own prayers and supplications they can also progress; more especially when they are the object of the intercession of the Holy Manifestations.[28]

The power of the soul in the next world

Looking again at the analogy of the unborn child, it is obvious that the many physical attributes being developed by the child in the womb are of little use to it while it is confined to that place. It is not until the birth and growth of the child that the value of those things becomes apparent. In a similar way, the spiritual powers of the soul will not be fully realized until it crosses over into the next world.

> Consider how a being, in the world of the womb, was deaf of ear and blind of eye, and mute of tongue; how he was bereft of any perceptions at all. But once, out of that world of darkness, he passed into this world of light, then his eye saw, his ear heard, his tongue spoke. In the same way, once he hath hastened away from this mortal place into the Kingdom of God, then he will be born in the spirit; then the eye of his perception will open, the ear of his soul will hearken, and all the truths of which he was ignorant before will be made plain and clear.[29]

Bahá'u'lláh explains that just as the womb restricts the unborn child, so too in this world the body restricts the 'tremendous power' of the soul:

> In like manner, every malady afflicting the body of man is an impediment that preventeth the soul from manifesting its inherent might and power. When it leaveth the body, however, it will evince such

ascendancy, and reveal such influence as no force on earth can equal. Every pure, every refined and sanctified soul will be endowed with tremendous power, and shall rejoice with exceeding gladness.[30]

Recognizing people in the next world

> As to the question whether the souls will recognize each other in the spiritual world: This (fact) is certain; for the Kingdom is the world of vision (i.e., things are visible in it), where all the concealed realities will become disclosed.[31]

'Abdu'l-Bahá states that after its passing, the soul will remember its life here. In a previous chapter it was explained that the inner powers of imagination, thought, comprehension and memory, being inherent powers of the soul, will remain part of man's spiritual reality when he is 'born' into the next world, and it is through these powers that souls will recognize each other in that world.

> And know thou for a certainty, that in the divine worlds, the spiritual beloved ones (believers) will recognize each other, and will seek union (with each other), but a spiritual union. Likewise, a love that one may have entertained for any one will not be forgotten in the world of the Kingdom. Likewise, thou wilt not forget (there) the life that thou hast had in the material world.[32]

Exactly how others in the next world will be recognized is a matter not given to us to know; 'Abdu'l-Bahá did, however, confirm that the soul retains its unique identity.

> . . . in the other world the human reality doth not assume a physical form, rather doth it take on a heavenly form, made up of elements of that heavenly realm.[33]

> This other and inner reality is called the heavenly body, the ethereal form which corresponds to this body.[34]

The human soul was called forth into the world of being by the operation of the power of the Word of God, a power which is beyond our comprehension, and it is this same power which leads those who seek spiritual truth to the place of understanding. Those who acquire this knowledge of their true selves become like pilgrims in this world, following a pathway through life which is signposted and illuminated by the Messenger of God. It is truly a knowledge which sets man free, since is satisfies the burning desire to discover meaning, to make sense of this world and to come to understand why we have appeared in it. Once that burden has been removed, then all of the pilgrim's energy can be focused on the journey of life and the acquisition of spiritual power through spiritual behaviour.

How this life is lived will ultimately determine the condition of the soul at that moment when it crosses over from this world into the spiritual worlds of God. Bahá'u'lláh revealed that:

> When the soul attaineth the Presence of God, it will assume the form that best befitteth its immortality and is worthy of its celestial habitation.[35]

CHAPTER 13

LIFE NOTES FOR THE PILGRIM

God, the All-Knowing, created the human soul and caused it to reflect a trace of the divine attributes; that is the true source of human power and the reason we are able to search, to discover the realities of things and to express the enormous potential of the mind. Man is born with a hunger to know. This is the brilliance of God's creation, that man, although imperfect in the beginning, has the capacity to acquire perfections, to acquire knowledge and to learn to appreciate beauty and harmony.

Over the past 50 years particularly, people's search for the meaning of life has resulted in hundreds of self-help books which have explored such subjects as 'positive thinking', 'mind power', 'goal-setting', 'problem-solving', 'controlling one's thoughts', 'fulfilling your potential', and so on. These books offer practical advice to those wishing to fulfil their personal goals, yet the majority of them are focused solely on the acquisition of wealth, no doubt because most people are primarily motivated by the promise of material rewards. Individuals who concentrate their life energies exclusively on material goals generally succeed in their ambitions and acquire the wealth they seek, and this is not surprising since the tremendous powers of the human soul can be focused on any number of ambitions. Every life has its crossroads and each one is free to choose which paths to take. However, those who wish to satisfy the yearnings of the soul must make it their first goal to know themselves – to discover those gems that God has deposited within their souls, and by doing so, begin the process of acquiring spiritual wealth.

The energizing effect of the revelation of the Word of God permeates throughout human society and, whether it is recognized immediately or not, the things which inspire people more often than not have their origin in spiritual principles and knowledge first revealed by the Messengers of God.

The divine art of goal-setting and being happy

The following brief selection of quotations from the Writings, which amount to spiritual counsels, aims to show that the knowledge springing from the Revealers of the Word of God is the foundation for all effective human endeavours, and the true source of happiness.

Choose your goals carefully

> O thou who art attracted to the Kingdom of God! Every soul seeketh an object and cherisheth a desire, and day and night striveth to attain his aim. One craveth riches, another thirsteth for glory and still another yearneth for fame, for art, for prosperity and the like. Yet finally all are doomed to loss and disappointment. One and all they leave behind them all that is theirs and empty-handed hasten to the realm beyond, and all their labours shall be in vain. To dust they shall all return, denuded, depressed, disheartened and in utter despair.
>
> But, praised be the Lord, thou art engaged in that which secureth for thee a gain that shall eternally endure; and that is naught but thine attraction to the Kingdom of God, thy faith, and thy knowledge, the enlightenment of thine heart, and thine earnest endeavour to promote the Divine Teachings.
>
> Verily this gift is imperishable and this wealth is a treasure from on high![1]

Focus on what is possible, not on your limitations

> The afflictions which come to humanity sometimes tend to centre the consciousness upon the limitations, and this is a veritable prison. Release comes by making of the will a Door through which the confirmations of the Spirit come.[2]

Aim for right action

> Our actions will help on the world, will spread civilization, will help the progress of science, and cause the arts to develop. Without action nothing in the material world can be accomplished, neither can words unaided advance a man in the spiritual Kingdom. It is not through

lip-service only that the elect of God have attained to holiness, but by patient lives of active service they have brought light into the world.

Therefore strive that your actions day by day may be beautiful prayers. Turn towards God, and seek always to do that which is right and noble. Enrich the poor, raise the fallen, comfort the sorrowful, bring healing to the sick, reassure the fearful, rescue the oppressed, bring hope to the hopeless, shelter the destitute![3]

Use the power of inner vision or insight

The spirit of man is itself informed and strengthened during meditation; through it affairs of which man knew nothing are unfolded before his view. Through it he receives Divine inspiration, through it he receives heavenly food.

Meditation is the key for opening the doors of mysteries. In that state man abstracts himself: in that state man withdraws himself from all outside objects; in that subjective mood he is immersed in the ocean of spiritual life and can unfold the secrets of things-in-themselves. To illustrate this, think of man as endowed with two kinds of sight; when the power of insight is being used the outward power of vision does not see.

This faculty of meditation frees man from the animal nature, discerns the reality of things, puts man in touch with God.

This faculty brings forth from the invisible plane the sciences and arts. Through the meditative faculty inventions are made possible, colossal undertakings are carried out; through it governments can run smoothly. Through this faculty man enters into the very Kingdom of God.

Nevertheless some thoughts are useless to man; they are like waves moving in the sea without result. But if the faculty of meditation is bathed in the inner light and characterized with divine attributes, the results will be confirmed.

The meditative faculty is akin to the mirror; if you put it before earthly objects it will reflect them. Therefore if the spirit of man is contemplating earthly subjects he will be informed of these.

But if you turn the mirror of your spirits heavenwards, the heavenly constellations and the rays of the Sun of Reality will be reflected in your hearts, and the virtues of the Kingdom will be obtained.

Therefore let us keep this faculty rightly directed – turning it to the heavenly Sun and not to earthly objects – so that we may discover the secrets of the Kingdom . . .[4]

Visualize your goals – see the end in the beginning

Look ye not upon the present, fix your gaze upon the times to come. In the beginning, how small is the seed, yet in the end it is a mighty tree. Look ye not upon the seed, look ye upon the tree, and its blossoms, and its leaves and its fruits.[5]

Don't waste time – act

How often have things been simple and easy of accomplishment, and yet most men have been heedless, and busied themselves with that which wasteth their time![6]

Accept that experiencing difficulties is a bounty

Verily God hath made adversity as a morning dew upon His green pasture, and a wick for His lamp which lighteth earth and heaven.[7]

Be not grieved; tests lead to the development of holy souls and the ardour of the flame of fire causeth the pure gold to shine and the violence of winds is conducive to the growth and thriving of a firm and well rooted tree.[8]

Be patient

So is the Kingdom of God. Consider the seed which was sown by Christ; verily, it did not blossom until after a long period. Thus it is incumbent upon thee to be patient in all affairs. Verily thy Lord is powerful, forgiving, precious and persevering! Depend upon the favour of thy Lord. He shall bless thee and protect thee under the shadow of His generosity and mercy.[9]

Everything of importance in this world demands the close attention of its seeker. The one in pursuit of anything must undergo difficulties and hardships until the object in view is attained and the great success is obtained. This is the case of things pertaining to the world . . . The seeker after the great guidance and eternal happiness necessarily will encounter difficulties. He must be patient under such circumstances.[10]

Be radiantly acquiescent

The confirmations of the Spirit are all those powers and gifts which some are born with (and which men sometimes call genius), but for which others have to strive with infinite pains. They come to that man or woman who accepts his life with radiant acquiescence.[11]

If thou wouldst hearken to my words, release thyself from the fetters of whatsoever cometh to pass. Nay rather, under all conditions thank thou thy loving Lord, and yield up thine affairs unto His Will that worketh as He pleaseth. This verily is better for thee than all else, in either world.[12]

Have faith in God

As ye have faith so shall your powers and blessings be. This is the balance – this is the balance – this is the balance.[13]

Far be it from us to despair at any time of the incalculable favours of God, for if it were His wish He could cause a mere atom to be transformed into a sun and a single drop into an ocean. He unlocketh thousands of doors, while man is incapable of conceiving even a single one.[14]

O thou who art turning thy face towards God! Close thine eyes to all things else, and open them to the realm of the All-Glorious. Ask whatsoever thou wishest of Him alone; seek whatsoever thou seekest from Him alone. With a look He granteth a hundred thousand hopes, with a glance He healeth a hundred thousand incurable ills, with a glimpse He layeth balm on every wound, with a nod He freeth the hearts from the shackles of grief. He doeth as He doeth, and what recourse have we? He carrieth out His Will, He ordaineth what He pleaseth. Then better for thee to bow down thy head in submission, and put thy trust in the All-Merciful Lord.[15]

CHAPTER 14

BAHÁ'U'LLÁH AND THE EVOLUTION OF SPIRITUAL MAN

Who is Bahá'u'lláh?

The pivotal message of Bahá'u'lláh's revelation is that religion is both cyclic and progressive. He Himself is the Prophet-Founder of the Bahá'í Faith, and the most recent of the great divine Messengers sent by God to man. Born in Iran on 12 November 1817, he grew up as Mírzá Ḥusayn-'Alí. Declaring Himself in 1863 to be the Messenger or 'Manifestation' of God for this age and to be the Promised One, the fulfilment of the prophecies of all past religions, the One who would through the power of His word establish a universal religion, He became known to the world as *Bahá'u'lláh* (The Glory of God).

A tremendous messianic fever gripped many religious communities during the first half of the 19th century. In Iran, amongst certain Shi'ah Muslims that sense of excitement was evident in their expectation that the return of the Twelfth Imam was imminent, while some Christian communities, such as the German Templers, became so convinced that the Messiah was about to appear that they travelled to Palestine to set up residence at the foot of Mount Carmel, God's holy mountain, to await His return.

Soon after His public declaration, Bahá'u'lláh was exiled from Iran by an increasingly fearful ruler influenced by an Islamic clergy that saw in this new revelation a threat to their own well-established positions in society. He was subsequently exiled further, from Baghdad to Istanbul (Constantinople), Adrianople and finally to 'Akká in Palestine, fulfilling the Old Testament prophecy which states:

In that day also he shall come even to thee from Assyria, and from the fortified cities, and from the fortress even to the river, and from sea to sea, and from mountain to mountain.¹

Bahá'u'lláh remained a prisoner in Palestine for the remainder of His life until His death in 1892. Towards the end of His life, he pitched His tent on the side of Mount Carmel, and revealed a Tablet there which in the most beautiful language refers to the birth of God's revelation within Him, and prophesies the establishment of His religion in that holy place.

Shoghi Effendi, the great-grandson of Bahá'u'lláh and the appointed Guardian of His Faith, wrote of His appearance in the world:

> To Israel He was neither more nor less than the incarnation of the 'Everlasting Father', the 'Lord of Hosts' come down 'with ten thousands of saints'; to Christendom Christ returned 'in the glory of the Father', to Shí'ah Islam the return of the Imám Husayn; to Sunni Islám the descent of the 'Spirit of God' (Jesus Christ); to the Zoroastrians the promised Sháh-Bahrám; to the Hindus the reincarnation of Krishna; to the Buddhists the fifth Buddha.²

Christians, who have been looking forward to the return of Christ for almost 2,000 years, should find the above statement thrilling, as should the followers of the other great world religions.

The essential unity of the Messengers of God

During His life Bahá'u'lláh revealed more than 100 volumes of writings and letters, among them the *Book of Certitude,* described by Shoghi Effendi as 'His pre-eminent doctrinal work'. In that book Bahá'u'lláh portrays the essential unity of all the Messengers or Prophets of God and explains in some detail the role played by them in the mystical relationship between God and man.

> These sanctified Mirrors, these Day-springs of ancient glory are one and all the Exponents on earth of Him Who is the central Orb of the universe, its Essence and ultimate Purpose. From Him proceed their knowledge and power; from Him is derived their sovereignty. The beauty of their countenance is but a reflection of His image, and their revelation a sign of His deathless glory. They are the Treasuries of divine

knowledge, and the Repositories of celestial wisdom. Through them is transmitted a grace that is infinite, and by them is revealed the light that can never fade.[3]

He also warned against discriminating between them.

> These attributes of God are not and have never been vouchsafed specially unto certain Prophets, and withheld from others. Nay, all the Prophets of God, His well-favoured, His holy, and chosen Messengers, are, without exception, the bearers of His names, and the embodiments of His attributes. They only differ in the intensity of their revelation, and the comparative potency of their light.[4]

Any differences ascribed to the Messengers of God by their followers is evidence only of man's limited comprehension of their essential and divine unity. Of course, in their outward appearance they did differ, but otherwise, the only distinguishing element between them lay in the measure of knowledge they were permitted by God to reveal to humanity during Their particular ministries.

Each one of them delivered teachings in accordance with the needs of man at the time they appeared, each performing a specific task within God's plan for the evolution of spiritual man.

> Every age hath its own problem, and every soul its particular aspiration. The remedy the world needeth in its present-day afflictions can never be the same as that which a subsequent age may require.[5]

The transformation of society

The appearance of the Messenger of God brings not only a spiritual renewal, it also signals a social renewal, because the knowledge He reveals becomes the cause of the transformation of society. A great spiritual energy is released into the world with the revelation of the Word of God, and it is that energy which shapes and prepares society, pushing humanity into the next stage of its evolution. In previous religious dispensations, in addition to the restatement of spiritual truths and codes of personal conduct, the Messengers of God have successively called for the establishment of unity in families, unity in tribes and unity in nationhood.

It is apparent today, however, that the process of nation-building has long since passed beyond the point where it can benefit humanity. What the world desperately needs now is for all nations and all peoples to recognize the truth that we are all one human family – a global community.

The establishment of a unified world community and ultimately a civilization based on spiritual principles is the primary social objective of Bahá'u'lláh's revelation. As the struggle to achieve that unity intensifies, no doubt more and more people will come to appreciate the statement made by Bahá'u'lláh towards the end of the 19th century that

> It is not for him to pride himself who loveth his own country, but rather for him who loveth the whole world. The earth is but one country, and mankind its citizens.[6]

The establishment of real unity and lasting peace among the nations of the world is the prize which humanity is so desperate to achieve, yet, while interdependence has increased and organizations such as the United Nations have come into being, the reality is that the community of nations has so far failed to establish an international body capable of delivering that prize. Until that happens, the safety and security of the world will remain uncertain.

Bahá'u'lláh's proclamation to the world

It has always been the task of the Messengers of God to stimulate the process of 'the evolution of spiritual man'[7] by setting the standard and calling humanity to lift its performance and to achieve its destiny. For example, the tribes of Israel responded to the call of Moses; the example of Christ's life and His teachings regarding love for others resulted in His message being spread around the world and transforming societies, while the Islamic civilization arising from Muhammad's revelation demonstrated the power of nationhood; it brought a wealth of new knowledge to man, became a shining light for the world and was ultimately the cause of the Renaissance in the West.

In the Bahá'í revelation, this most recent episode in the spiritual life of humanity, Bahá'u'lláh set the standard in a significant proclamation to the then kings and rulers of the world over the years 1867–1868. In a series of strongly worded letters to such figures as Queen Victoria, Sultan

'Abdu'l-'Azíz, Czar Alexander II, Kaiser Wilhelm I, Emperor Franz Joseph, Napoleon III and Pope Pius IX, he proclaimed His mission and challenged those leaders to bring unity to the nations of the world by establishing what He called the Most Great Peace. He called on them to reduce their armaments, to stop taxing their citizens for that purpose and to introduce a wide range of changes in their countries which would promote the oneness of humanity and encourage the establishment of a spiritual civilization. Regrettably, His summons was either ignored or rejected and that response set the stage for what Shoghi Effendi would later refer to as 'a retributory calamity and an act of holy and supreme discipline'.[8]

Shoghi Effendi's sobering assessment in 1940 of the situation then facing humanity still seems entirely applicable today, 70 years later:

> Humanity has, alas, with increasing insistence, preferred, instead of acknowledging and adoring the Spirit of God as embodied in His religion in this day, to worship those false idols, untruths and half-truths, which are obscuring its religions, corrupting its spiritual life, convulsing its political institutions, corroding its social fabric, and shattering its economic structure.[9]

His vision of the future, however, was very bright. He explained that just as the suffering which individuals endure bears fruit in the end, so too will the disciplining process which humanity must go through ultimately produce a 'world-embracing Fellowship':

> . . . the radical transformation of human society; the rolling up of the present-day Order; the fundamental changes affecting the structure of government; the weakening of the pillars of religion; the rise of dictatorships; the spread of tyranny; the fall of monarchies; the decline of ecclesiastical institutions; the increase of anarchy and chaos; the extension and consolidation of the Movement of the Left; the fanning into flame of the smouldering fire of racial strife; the development of infernal engines of war; the burning of cities; the contamination of the atmosphere of the earth – these stand out as the signs and portents that must either herald or accompany the retributive calamity which, as decreed by Him Who is the Judge and Redeemer of mankind, must, sooner or later, afflict a society which, for the most part, and for over a century, has turned a deaf ear to the Voice of God's Messenger in this

day – a calamity which must purge the human race of the dross of its age-long corruptions, and weld its component parts into a firmly-knit world-embracing Fellowship – a Fellowship destined, in the fullness of time, to be incorporated in the framework, and to be galvanized by the spiritualizing influences, of a mysteriously expanding, divinely appointed Order, and to flower, in the course of future Dispensations, into a Civilization, the like of which mankind has, at no stage in its evolution, witnessed.[10]

The condition of society

> And yet, is not the object of every Revelation to effect a transformation in the whole character of mankind, a transformation that shall manifest itself both outwardly and inwardly, that shall affect both its inner life and external conditions? For if the character of mankind be not changed, the futility of God's universal Manifestations would be apparent.[11]

The present condition of humanity calls urgently for such a transformation. Material progress has consistently outstripped spiritual development. The great numbers of wars and conflicts that have occurred, and the enormously destructive power of the new technologies and weapons used, has resulted in loss of life and suffering beyond belief. Bahá'u'lláh foresaw the pain and conflict ahead and lamented the fact. In a particularly moving passage He wrote,

> How long will humanity persist in its waywardness? How long will injustice continue? How long is chaos and confusion to reign amongst men? How long will discord agitate the face of society? . . . The winds of despair are, alas, blowing from every direction, and the strife that divideth and afflicteth the human race is daily increasing. The signs of impending convulsions and chaos can now be discerned, inasmuch as the prevailing order appeareth to be lamentably defective.[12]

He likened the world to a severely ill patient standing in need of healing, and stated that those claiming to know the remedy to its sickness have succeeded only in making its condition worse.

Regard the world as the human body which, though at its creation whole and perfect, hath been afflicted, through various causes, with grave disorders and maladies. Not for one day did it gain ease, nay, its sickness waxed more severe, as it fell under the treatment of ignorant physicians, who gave full rein to their personal desires, and have erred grievously.[13]

Witness how the world is being afflicted with a fresh calamity every day. Its tribulation is continually deepening . . . At one time it hath been agitated by contentions and disputes, at another it hath been convulsed by wars, and fallen a victim to inveterate diseases. Its sickness is approaching the stage of utter hopelessness, inasmuch as the true Physician is debarred from administering the remedy, whilst unskilled practitioners are regarded with favour, and are accorded full freedom to act.[14]

Divine Physicians

Bahá'u'lláh states categorically that *only* the Manifestations of God are capable of making a suitable diagnosis of the conditions affecting the world of humanity.

To none is given the right to question their words or disparage their conduct, for they are the only ones who can claim to have understood the patient and to have correctly diagnosed its ailments. No man, however acute his perception, can ever hope to reach the heights which the wisdom and understanding of the Divine Physician have attained.[15]

It is they, He says, who prescribe the correct remedies according to the needs of humanity at the time in which they appear. The force required to achieve the transformation of human society is born of the Word of God which they reveal. Bahá'u'lláh writes:

The All-Knowing Physician hath His finger on the pulse of mankind. He perceiveth the disease, and prescribeth, in His unerring wisdom, the remedy.[16]

The Prophets of God should be regarded as physicians whose task is to foster the well-being of the world and its peoples . . .[17]

The remedy

The divine prescription to remedy the present condition of humanity can be found in the following words of Bahá'u'lláh:

> The well-being of mankind, its peace and security, are unattainable unless and until its unity is firmly established.[18]

And its unity, He declares, is to be realized through religion, 'the changeless Faith of God, eternal in the past, eternal in the future'.[19] The renewal of religion and the acceptance of the oneness of mankind remains the only power capable of establishing peace and unity.

Throughout His writings, Bahá'u'lláh refers frequently to the essential unity underlying all religions, and demonstrates that it is only man who has made them become a cause of division and disharmony. The distortion by its followers of the true heart of each of the past religions has led to the existing disunity between faiths, which in turn, lies at the root of all human conflict. 'Abdu'l-Bahá stated:

> For after all, the earth is but the everlasting graveyard, the vast, universal cemetery of all mankind. Yet men fight to possess this graveyard, waging war and battle, killing each other. What ignorance! How spacious the earth is with room in plenty for all! How thoughtful the providence which has so allotted that every man may derive his sustenance from it! . . . Fundamentally, all warfare and bloodshed in the human world are due to the lack of unity between the religions, which through superstitions and adherence to theological dogmas have obscured the one reality which is the source and basis of them all.[20]

Bringing peace to humanity through religion may seem to be a formidable if not impossible task, yet this is precisely what Bahá'u'lláh prescribed. He said,

> Religion is the greatest of all means for the establishment of order in the world and for the peaceful contentment of all that dwell therein.[21]

and again,

> That which the Lord hath ordained as the sovereign remedy and mightiest instrument for the healing of all the world is the union of all its peoples in one universal Cause, one common Faith. This can in no wise be achieved except through the power of a skilled, an all-powerful and inspired Physician.[22]

'Strive, therefore', He advises, 'to save its life through the wholesome medicine which the almighty hand of the unerring Physician hath prepared.'[23]

A change such as the world has not yet experienced

The expectations implied in Bahá'u'lláh's prescription for the world are far-reaching by any standards. Shoghi Effendi summarizes them in statements such as these:

> The emergence of a world community, the consciousness of world citizenship, the founding of a world civilization and culture . . .[24]

In many of his writings he makes it clear that the Order established by Bahá'u'lláh will be the vehicle for this radical transformation in the structure of society, and to those who would look upon the achievement of such objectives as wishful thinking he addresses this resounding statement:

> Let there be no mistake. The principle of the Oneness of Mankind – the pivot round which all the teachings of Bahá'u'lláh revolve – is no mere outburst of ignorant emotionalism or an expression of vague and pious hope . . . It does not constitute merely the enunciation of an ideal, but stands inseparably associated with an institution adequate to embody its truth, demonstrate its validity, and perpetuate its influence.[25]

The healing of the world

Bahá'u'lláh's teachings offer a comprehensive solution to the major problems facing mankind today, and while many people may have heard of Bahá'u'lláh or heard of the Bahá'í Faith, they probably do not comprehend how significant its claims are, or appreciate what a vital role it is destined to play in humanity's immediate future.

Historically, the vitality of religions gradually wanes, the purity of their teachings having become obscured by the introduction of man-made doctrines and trappings which bear no relationship to their original spiritual message. It is this situation which calls forth the divine response in the form of a new Messenger of God. Bahá'u'lláh made it clear that the renewal of the religion of God must play a pivotal role in healing the wounds in society and establishing peace in the world. This renewal is a spiritual springtime containing within itself the power to achieve this goal.

The fact that the corruption of religion has contributed to much of the conflict still going on in the world today cannot be denied, but when we look back at those times when the Messengers of God appeared in our midst, we can also see that religion can change people, transform societies, affect laws and morality and become a unifying force. Today we are living again in such a time. Through Bahá'u'lláh, God has intervened once again in the life of humanity.

Bahá'u'lláh states emphatically that what the world *needs* now is *unity*. Wars have not brought unity. The many different systems of government have all been shown to have shortcomings. The various economic strategies tried to date have failed. Why? Because these great challenges we face are universal in nature and must be dealt with by all the peoples of the world acting together.

Time has also become an issue, since there are a number of important questions that humanity must find answers for very soon. For instance,

- How will the natural resources of the planet be protected?

- How should the common lifeline of the planet's fresh water be managed?

- How will the issue of starvation and extreme poverty in certain nations be resolved?

- How will the problem of contamination of the earth's atmosphere be remedied?

- How are the problems of conflict and terrorism to be addressed in the 21st century?

These are world problems requiring world solutions. These problems cry out for the creation of a world body which is universally accepted and supported, capable of dealing effectively with these crises. Technology has shrunk the world into a 'global village', yet we still have over 150 independent nation states, all fiercely protective of their own sovereign rights, when what is needed – *the price of peace* – is that all nations should give up at least some of their national sovereignty in favour of establishing not only a world government, but a world civilization.

This is the standard that has been set by the Messenger of God for this day. Bahá'u'lláh has given us this vision, a comprehensive vision of the evolution of human society which enables us to see the various peoples of the world as one human family, and the various religions in the history of mankind as one religion – the religion of God – not separated from each other, but connected to each other; all of them stemming from the same divine source, and each one building on the religion preceding it.

The consequences of failing to act

While Bahá'u'lláh referred to the great civilizing influence that religion has on human society, He also warned that 'should the lamp of religion be obscured, chaos and confusion will ensue'.[26] In the absence of the protective influence of true religion which embodies the love of God, various cancers have afflicted the body of mankind, one of those cancers being materialism.

> It is this same cancerous materialism, born originally in Europe, carried to excess in the North American continent, contaminating the Asiatic peoples and nations, spreading its ominous tentacles to the borders of Africa, and now invading its very heart, which Bahá'u'lláh in unequivocal and emphatic language denounced in His Writings, comparing it to a devouring flame and regarding it as the chief factor in precipitating the dire ordeals and world-shaking crises that must necessarily involve the burning of cities and the spread of terror and consternation in the hearts of men.[27]

The physical consequences of rampant materialism are clearly evident in the enormous toll it has taken on the resources of the entire planet; the spiritual consequences are even worse and are reflected in the degenerating behaviour amongst people and the deepening climate of oppression in society.

> The perversion of human nature, the degradation of human conduct, the corruption and dissolution of human institutions . . . the voice of human conscience is stilled, the sense of decency and shame is obscured, conceptions of duty, of solidarity, of reciprocity and loyalty are distorted, and the very feeling of peacefulness, of joy and of hope is gradually extinguished.[28]

When God is ignored in the ordering of human affairs, the consequences are grim, and Bahá'u'lláh throughout His writings used the most sobering language to depict the spiritually bankrupt condition of humanity.

Today, every form of media is to some degree reflecting the truth that millions of people are finding it increasingly difficult to live, grow and flourish in the world's present environment. To remedy this situation, Bahá'u'lláh has issued a challenge to humanity, and that challenge is to accept the pivotal principle of the age, namely, *recognition of the oneness of mankind*.

There is no doubt that the new world order envisioned by Bahá'u'lláh will eventually emerge as a result of the great spiritual forces released by His revelation; the world will undergo a gradual transformation from disunited interdependence into a mutually supporting and united global community, but how quickly it happens and how much suffering humanity will have to endure in the meantime will depend on how soon all nations and all peoples begin to embrace the principle of the oneness of mankind.

No-one doubts that the existing technology can administer a complex international community of nations, but so far the lack of unity in the world prevents this goal from becoming a reality. What is becoming increasingly clear is that the existing state of affairs is utterly inadequate for the needs of humanity today, and this is reflected in the steadily worsening condition of the planet. Shoghi Effendi referred to this as 'the process of general disintegration – a process that must necessarily precede the fundamental reconstruction of human society'.[29]

An organic change

The prospect of the emergence of a new world order is very exciting since the transformation required of society will affect all aspects of life. Nothing will remain as it was before; Shoghi Effendi stated, 'It implies an organic change in the structure of present-day society, a change such as the world has not yet experienced . . . It represents the consummation of human evolution . . .'[30]

These changes in the material and spiritual life of humanity are inevitable, since ultimately the creative power of the Word of God is an irresistible force in the world. Bahá'u'lláh writes:

> The utterance of God is a lamp, whose light is these words: Ye are the fruits of one tree, and the leaves of one branch. Deal ye one with another with the utmost love and harmony, with friendliness and fellowship. He Who is the Day Star of Truth beareth Me witness! So powerful is the light of unity that it can illuminate the whole earth. The one true God, He Who knoweth all things, Himself testifieth to the truth of these words.[31]

Although the present state of human society is still far from the standard called for by the Messenger of God, the Writings promise that God's purpose for humanity, the consummation of the great process of maturation initiated so long ago, cannot be stopped; its progress is inevitable. Adib Taherzadeh summarizes the unfoldment of this process:

> The spirit of the age released by Bahá'u'lláh may be likened to forces which press hard upon humanity and drive it towards universality and the oneness of mankind. When people, whether consciously or unconsciously, oppose these forces, they create tensions within their societies. Like a tidal wave as it gathers momentum, the magnitude of the forces released by Bahá'u'lláh is increasing day by day and consequently there will come a time when these tensions reach breaking-point.
>
> Almost every war or distressing event which has happened on this planet in the last hundred years has been caused by man's opposition to the forces of universality and unity which have been influencing the world since the coming of Bahá'u'lláh.[32]

Humanity's coming of age

Ultimately that wave of spiritual energy will overcome the obstacles in its path, and turn humanity towards unity. In Shoghi Effendi's brilliant work *The Promised Day is Come*, we find an inspiring portrayal of the bright future destined for humanity:

> The ages of its infancy and childhood are past, never again to return, while the Great Age, the consummation of all ages, which must signalize the coming of age of the entire human race, is yet to come. The convulsions of this transitional and most turbulent period in the annals of humanity are the essential prerequisites, and herald the inevitable approach, of that Age of Ages, 'the time of the end', in which the folly and tumult of strife that has, since the dawn of history, blackened the annals of mankind, will have been finally transmuted into the wisdom and the tranquillity of an undisturbed, a universal, and lasting peace, in which the discord and separation of the children of men will have given way to the worldwide reconciliation, and the complete unification of the divers elements that constitute human society.
>
> This will indeed be the fitting climax of that process of integration which, starting with the family, the smallest unit in the scale of human organization, must, after having called successively into being the tribe, the city-state, and the nation, continue to operate until it culminates in the unification of the whole world, the final object and the crowning glory of human evolution on this planet. It is this stage which humanity, willingly or unwillingly, is resistlessly approaching. It is for this stage that this vast, this fiery ordeal which humanity is experiencing is mysteriously paving the way. It is with this stage that the fortunes and the purpose of the Faith of Bahá'u'lláh are indissolubly linked. It is the creative energies which His Revelation has released . . . that have instilled into humanity the capacity to attain this final stage in its organic and collective evolution.[33]

This reference to the coming of age of humanity leads us, finally, to examine the phenomenon of 'universal cycles' – the ultimate process involving the body of mankind, and one which puts its present condition into perspective.

Universal cycles and the evolution of spiritual man

One of the longest and greatest of the many processes going on in the world is referred to in the Writings as 'universal cycles'. Just as the human soul gradually evolves and acquires qualities and attributes throughout this life, so also over a much longer period does human society evolve, becoming more complex, more unified, reflecting increasing degrees of perfection, and it is the Messengers of God who progressively stimulate this process of maturation in the human kingdom. Their appearance advances the life of human society by transforming the lives of the individuals within it. 'Abdu'l-Bahá states:

> Briefly, there were many universal cycles preceding this one in which we are living. They were consummated, completed and their traces obliterated. The divine and creative purpose in them was the evolution of spiritual man, just as it is in this cycle. The circle of existence is the same circle; it returns. The tree of life has ever borne the same heavenly fruit.[34]

> When a cycle is ended, a new cycle begins; and the old one, on account of the great events which take place, is completely forgotten, and not a trace or record of it will remain. As you see, we have no records of twenty thousand years ago, although we have before proved by argument that life on this earth is very ancient. It is not one hundred thousand, or two hundred thousand, or one million or two million years old; it is very ancient, and the ancient records and traces are entirely obliterated.[35]

These statements reveal that the physical world is merely the stage upon which the drama of material and spiritual evolution has been re-enacted before. On the one hand this information is quite astounding; on the other hand, it is very much in line with all that we have read up until now, that is, that there has always been a creation, that God's bounty has never ceased, that the Messengers of God have always appeared from the heaven of God's will, and that the evolution of spiritual man is an ongoing process.

We know nothing about those universal cycles which have preceded this current cycle and this is confirmed by Bahá'u'lláh in His statement:

That no records concerning them are now available, should be attributed to their extreme remoteness, as well as to the vast changes which the earth hath undergone since their time.[36]

How astonishing to think that great cycles of existence and development have happened before; how marvellous to realize that everything we see and experience in this material world has come about for one great purpose, namely, the evolution of spiritual man, and how uplifting to apprehend that we are linked to the creative force behind all existence in such a meaningful way, that we are led to gradually manifest powers and perfections whose origins are beyond this world.

Evolutionary process – the principle of gradual development

> Man must walk in many paths and be subjected to various processes in his evolution upward.[37]

Here again, 'Abdu'l-Bahá uses the analogy of the seed and then the embryo to emphasize the principle that gradual growth and development is 'the universal divine organization and the natural system'.[38]

> Each seed has in it from the first all the vegetable perfections . . . but not visibly; afterward little by little they appear. So it is first the shoot which appears from the seed, then the branches, leaves, blossoms and fruits; but from the beginning of its existence all these things are in the seed, potentially, though not apparently.
>
> In the same way, the embryo possesses from the first all perfections, such as the spirit, the mind, the sight, the smell, the taste – in one word, all the powers – but they are not visible and become so only by degrees.
>
> Similarly, the terrestrial globe from the beginning was created with all its elements, substances, minerals, atoms and organisms; but these only appeared by degrees: first the mineral, then the plant, afterward the animal, and finally man. But from the first these kinds and species existed, but were undeveloped in the terrestrial globe, and then appeared only gradually. For the supreme organization of God, and the universal natural system, surround all beings, and all are subject to this rule. When you consider this universal system, you see that there

is not one of the beings which at its coming into existence has reached the limit of perfection. No, they gradually grow and develop, and then attain the degree of perfection.[39]

The above explanations emphasize to man the requirement for patience in all of his affairs. The physical characteristics of the embryo appear only gradually; similarly, the acquisition of spiritual qualities takes time. This same principle of gradual development applies to the spiritualization of the human race. Life is a process, maturation is a process and there are no shortcuts. Fortunately, however, man has been given the most potent aid in the form of the Word of God, the power which can uplift human society by transforming the individuals within it. That is why Bahá'u'lláh described the laws and teachings contained in His Revelation as marvellous gifts to be embraced and savoured by humanity:

> Think not that We have revealed unto you a mere code of laws. Nay, rather, We have unsealed the choice Wine with the fingers of might and power.[40]

> Indeed His ordinances constitute the mightiest stronghold for the protection of the world and the safeguarding of its peoples . . .[41]

The Bahá'ís

The word *Bahá* means light, or glory; hence, *Bahá'u'lláh* is translated as 'The Glory of God' and to be a *Bahá'í* is to be a follower of the light.

The Messengers of God are like different lamps that have appeared periodically to guide humanity to the knowledge of God, but the light they have shed has been the same light. A Bahá'í, therefore, is someone who accepts the divine origin of all the Prophets of God, and has recognized that light in the person of Bahá'u'lláh, the most recent in a line of Prophets stretching back far into the past.

Bahá'ís are a worldwide community of people from every background who have made a commitment to try to live their lives according to the teachings of Bahá'u'lláh, to gradually transform themselves to reflect a more spiritual view of the human reality and of human society. Some come from other religious backgrounds, while others have come to the Faith in spite of never having been previously taught about God or religion. What they all have in common is a desire to find meaning in their personal lives, as well as a desire to help create a better world and to be world citizens. Bahá'ís are a global community who promote the oneness of God, the oneness of religion and the oneness of humanity.

It is always far easier to talk about or write about high ideals and spiritual qualities than it is to live up to them, and choosing to become a Bahá'í does not automatically make the goal of transforming oneself less difficult, it simply signals the desire to begin that process.

There are now Bahá'í communities in towns and cities in most parts of the world.

Bahá'ís do not proselytize or seek to create 'converts'; rather, they offer the knowledge of their Faith to those who are seeking it, inviting them to participate to the level they wish. Every soul has the capacity to acquire the knowledge of God, and Bahá'ís are happy to provide the opportunity for people to explore the Writings and to decide for themselves. These opportunities generally take the form of study circles in which interested people join a small group of Bahá'ís to read and discuss the Writings. In addition, there are regular devotional meetings in most communities, open to all, where people are invited to say prayers and read the Words of God.

EPILOGUE

A TRIBUTE TO MY PARENTS

I like to imagine that everyone gets to a point in their lives when they begin to think seriously about 'the meaning of life', and pause to write down their thoughts and observations. Perhaps most will not, but then many write a Will, which shows that they have spent at least some time thinking about their life and its conclusion.

For me, the subjects of life and life after death have never been far from my thoughts, even as a child. Why? Probably because my parents were deeply religious people with strongly held beliefs on these matters . . . beliefs that they impressed upon their three sons.

Part of learning about yourself involves coming to understand your parents. The parents I grew up with were not particularly young people. My mother was already in her 40s when I was born, with greying hair and a face beautifully etched by an extraordinarily rich palette of life experiences – hers a canvas tinted by raw, rural Australia; nursing training; studying music (piano) at the Melbourne Conservatory; then by hard years in the Australian Army traversing the deserts of North Africa, nursing wounded soldiers of the 8th Army during the 1939–1945 War. After the war she went to Indonesia as a nurse/missionary, but returned to Australia when the situation in that country deteriorated. In 1952 she married my father and soon after they left as missionaries to the Gulf region of Papua New Guinea.

My father was two years younger than my mother, and had also been through life-changing experiences, such as the Great Depression of the 1930s, parents who divorced, his embracing of fundamentalist Christianity, service in the Medical Corps of the New Zealand Division of the 8th Army in North Africa, and after the war, Bible Institute with studies in linguistics leading to a commitment to becoming a missionary in Papua New Guinea.

I include these thumbnail biographies to show that they had both no doubt already examined their own feelings about life and death . . . the experience of leaving your homeland to travel to a distant theatre of war would magnify any thoughts you might have about your own mortality and no doubt they communicated those attitudes to me as I was growing up. There are no further opportunities to ask them about it now, because they have both advanced to the next world, but I am thankful for what they imparted to me when I was young; they believed in God, they spoke about spiritual matters and about life and death, and through their training and instruction steered me towards seeking spiritual truth. I shall always be grateful to them for this, because I have since come to realize that today in the midst of a society that has largely turned away from seeking spiritual truth, such an upbringing is becoming something of a rarity.

I am also thankful for the many wonderful people whose paths I have crossed. To link up with you and travel together for a while has made the road easier and the journey more delightful, and convinced me that the way we spend the time we have together in this world is a significant element in our preparation for the next world.

How amazing to think that when we have crossed over, generations yet unborn will follow us through this testing place, the world, and they too will laugh and cry, experience pain and joy as they gather to themselves the powers, the qualities and the attributes that are the currency of eternity.

The natural inclination of parents is to protect their children from any kind of suffering, in the belief that such action will ensure their happiness in this world, when actually the hurts and pains associated with this life are inevitable and contribute to the attainment of maturity and the acquisition of worthy attributes.

Of course, parents will always be there to support their children, to love and care for them, but we must also accept that in the process of trying to shield them from pain, we may also be denying them the opportunities to grow stronger in themselves. The process of purifying gold by burning off the dross requires intense heat and the forming of good character is no different. In order to discover the true self, every person must face the tests prepared by the Assayer of souls to ready that soul for the journey ahead.

To dear Lilian and Nigel who launched me on my journey – thank you for your love and care; I know I didn't say that enough while you were still here.

Geoff

GLOSSARY

The Báb 1819–1850. Prophet-Founder of the Bábí Faith, who appeared immediately before Bahá'u'lláh, and prepared the people to recognize Him when He proclaimed His mission.

Bahá'u'lláh 1817–1892. Prophet-Founder of the Bahá'í Faith.

'Abdu'l-Bahá 1844–1921. Eldest son of Bahá'u'lláh, appointed by Him to be the authorized interpreter of His Writings, and the Centre of His Covenant.

Shoghi Effendi 1897–1957. Great-grandson of Bahá'u'lláh, grandson of 'Abdu'l-Bahá and appointed by Him to be the Guardian of the Bahá'í Faith upon His passing, to perpetuate the Covenant of succession and to fulfil the role of divinely authorized interpreter of the Writings.

The Writings In this book, refers to the Bahá'í Writings.

Evolution In this book the word *evolution* is used in accordance with the definition given to it by 'Abdu'l-Bahá, that

1. the earth was created 'with all its elements, substances, minerals, atoms and organisms; but these only appeared by degrees: first the mineral, then the plant, afterward the animal, and finally man;' and that

2. 'from the first these kinds and species existed, but were

undeveloped in the terrestrial globe, and then appeared only gradually'.

This contrasts with Darwinian theory, since the Bahá'í view of evolution teaches that all species were created potentially complete from the first, and although they may have changed form, they never lost their unique identity, having all gone through a gradual process of growth and development before reaching the limit of their perfections. Similarly, in the spiritual sense, *evolution* is used to describe the gradual realization within the human species of the great potential latent in it and which has always existed.

BIBLIOGRAPHY

'Abdu'l-Bahá. *'Abdu'l-Bahá in London* (1912, 1921). London: Bahá'í Publishing Trust, 1982.

— *'Abdu'l-Bahá on Divine Philosophy.* Comp. I. F. Chamberlain. Boston: The Tudor Press, 1918.

— *Foundations of World Unity.* Wilmette, IL: Bahá'í Publishing Trust, 1968.

— *Memorials of the Faithful.* Trans. M. Gail. Wilmette, IL: Bahá'í Publishing Trust, 1971.

— *Paris Talks: Addresses given by 'Abdu'l-Bahá in 1911* (1912). London: Bahá'í Publishing Trust, 12th ed. 1995.

— *The Promulgation of Universal Peace: Talks Delivered by 'Abdu'l-Baha During His Visit to the United States and Canada in 1912* (1922, 1925). Comp. H. MacNutt. Wilmette, IL: Bahá'í Publishing Trust, 2nd ed. 1982.

— *The Secret of Divine Civilization.* Trans. M. Gail. Wilmette, IL: Bahá'í Publishing Trust, 1957.

— *Selections from the Writings of 'Abdu'l-Bahá.* Comp. Research Department of the Universal House of Justice. Haifa: Bahá'í World Centre, 1978.

— *Some Answered Questions* (1908). Comp. L. Clifford Barney. Wilmette, IL: Bahá'í Publishing Trust, 3rd ed. 1981.

— *Tablets of Abdul-Baha Abbas.* 3 vols. Chicago: Bahá'í Publishing Society, 1909–1916.

— *Tablets of the Divine Plan.* Wilmette, IL: Bahá'í Publishing Trust, 1975.

— 'Tablet to Dr. Auguste Henri Forel', in *The Bahá'í World 1968–1973*, vol. XV, pp. 37–43.

— *A Traveler's Narrative Written to Illustrate the Episode of the Báb* (1891). Trans. E. G. Browne. Wilmette, IL: Bahá'í Publishing Trust, rev. ed. 1980.

The Báb. *Selections from the Writings of the Báb.* Comp. Research Department of the Universal House of Justice. Haifa: Bahá'í World Centre, 1976.

Bahá'í Prayers: A Selection of Prayers Revealed by Bahá'u'lláh, The Báb, and 'Abdu'l-Bahá. Wilmette, IL: Bahá'í Publishing Trust, rev. ed. 1991.

Bahai Scriptures: Selections from the Utterances of Baha'u'llah and Abdul Baha. Ed. Horace Holley. New York: Brentano's, 1923.

The Bahá'í World: An International Record. Vol. XV, Haifa: Bahá'í World Centre, 1976; vol. XVIII, Haifa: Bahá'í World Centre, 1986.

Bahá'í World Faith: Selected Writings of Bahá'u'lláh and 'Abdu'l-Bahá. Wilmette, IL: Bahá'í Publishing Trust, rev. ed. 1956.

Bahá'u'lláh. *Epistle to the Son of the Wolf.* Trans. Shoghi Effendi. Wilmette, IL: Bahá'í Publishing Trust, rev. ed. 1976.

— *Gems of Divine Mysteries: Javáhiru'l-Asrár.* Haifa: Bahá'í World Centre, 2002.

— *Gleanings from the Writings of Bahá'u'lláh.* Trans. Shoghi Effendi. Wilmette, IL: Bahá'í Publishing Trust, 2nd ed. 1976.

— *The Hidden Words of Bahá'u'lláh.* Trans. Shoghi Effendi. Wilmette, IL: Bahá'í Publishing Trust, 1970; New Delhi: Bahá'í Publishing Trust, 1987.

— *The Kitáb-i-Aqdas: The Most Holy Book.* Haifa: Bahá'í World Centre, 1992.

— *Kitáb-i-Íqán: The Book of Certitude.* Trans. Shoghi Effendi. Wilmette, IL: Bahá'í Publishing Trust, 2nd ed. 1950.

— *Prayers and Meditations by Bahá'u'lláh.* Trans. Shoghi Effendi. Wilmette, IL: Bahá'í Publishing Trust, 1938, 1987.

— *The Seven Valleys and the Four Valleys.* Trans. M. Gail with A.-K. Khan. Wilmette, IL: Bahá'í Publishing Trust, rev. ed. 1975.

— *The Summons of the Lord of Hosts: Tablets of Bahá'u'lláh.* Haifa: Bahá'í World Centre, 2002.

— *Tablets of Bahá'u'lláh Revealed after the Kitáb-i-Aqdas.* Comp. Research Department of the Universal House of Justice. Haifa: Bahá'í World Centre, 1978.

Bible. *Holy Bible.* King James version. London: Eyre and Spottiswoode, various dates.

Church, F. J. (trans.) *Trial and Death of Socrates.* London, New York: Macmillan, 1890.

The Compilation of Compilations. Prepared by the Universal House of Justice 1963–1990. 2 vols. Sydney: Bahá'í Publications Australia, 1991.

The Divine Art of Living: Selections from Writings of Bahá'u'lláh and 'Abdu'l-Bahá. Comp. M. H. Paine. Wilmette, IL: Bahá'í Publishing Trust, 4th rev. ed. 1979.

Lights of Guidance: A Bahá'í Reference File. Comp. H. Hornby. New Delhi: Bahá'í Publishing Trust, 1983.

Maxwell, May. *An Early Pilgrimage* (1917). Oxford: George Ronald, rev. ed. 1969.

Qur'án. *The Koran.* Trans. J. M. Rodwell. New York: Dutton, 1971.

Shoghi Effendi. *Arohanui: Letters from Shoghi Effendi to New Zealand.* Suva, Fiji: Bahá'í Publishing Trust, 1982.

— *Citadel of Faith: Messages to America, 1947–1957.* Wilmette, IL: Bahá'í Publishing Trust, 1965.

— *God Passes By* (1944). Wilmette, IL: Bahá'í Publishing Trust, rev. ed. 1974.

— *Messages to the Bahá'í World 1950–1957.* Wilmette, IL: Bahá'í Publishing Trust, 2nd ed. 1971.

— *The Promised Day Is Come* (1941). Wilmette, IL: Bahá'í Publishing Trust, rev. ed. 1980.

— *The World Order of Bahá'u'lláh: Selected Letters by Shoghi Effendi* (1938). Wilmette, IL: Bahá'í Publishing Trust, 2nd rev. ed. 1974.

— *Unfolding Destiny: The Messages from the Guardian of the Bahá'í Faith to the Bahá'í Community of the British Isles*. London: Bahá'í Publishing Trust, 1981.

Star of the West: The Bahai Magazine. Periodical, 25 vols. 1910–1935. Vols. 1–14 RP Oxford: George Ronald, 1978. Complete CD-ROM version: Talisman Educational Software/Special Ideas, 2001.

Taherzadeh, Adib. *The Covenant of Bahá'u'lláh*. Oxford: George Ronald, 1992.

— *The Revelation of Bahá'u'lláh*. 4 vols. Oxford: George Ronald, 1974–1987.

NOTES AND REFERENCES

Why this book?
1 *Church, Trial and Death of Socrates*, p. 129.
2 ibid. p. 112.
3 ibid. p. 90.
4 ibid. p. 115.
5 ibid. p. 121.
6 Bahá'u'lláh, quoted by Shoghi Effendi, *The Promised Day Is Come*, pp. 112–13.
7 A researcher announced in February 2001 that the human genome contained only 30,000 genes, and that figure was recently reduced further to around 25,000. As it turns out, this is approximately twice the number of genes possessed by a worm or a fruit fly. Many concluded that this number was too few to explain the incredible diversity of human behaviour and that, therefore, our genetic inheritance had to be far less important to what we are than the various external influences.
8 'Abdu'l-Bahá, *Promulgation of Universal Peace*, p. 89.
9 Bahá'u'lláh, *Hidden Words*, Arabic no. 32.
10 'Abdu'l-Bahá, *Some Answered Questions*, no. 81, pp. 283–5. See pp. 282–9 for the full text.
11 Bahá'u'lláh, Lawḥ-i-Maqṣúd, in *Tablets*, p. 173.

1 These brief moments
1 'Abdu'l-Bahá, *Selections*, no. 110, pp. 135–6.
2 'Abdu'l-Bahá, *Paris Talks*, no. 23, p. 68.
3 Bahá'u'lláh, *Hidden Words*, Persian no. 75.
4 Jas. 4:14.

2 The limits of understanding
1 'Abdu'l-Bahá, *Selections*, no. 24. p. 54.
2 'Abdu'l-Bahá, 'Tablet to Dr. Auguste Henri Forel', in *The Bahá'í World*, vol. 15, p. 40.
3 Dan. 12:9.
4 John 16:12–13.
5 'Abdu'l-Bahá, *Some Answered Questions*, no. 3, p. 7.
6 'Abdu'l-Bahá, *Promulgation*, p. 424. See pp. 423–5 for the complete text.
7 'Abdu'l-Bahá, *Selections*, no. 21, pp. 48–9.
8 'Abdu'l-Bahá, *Promulgation*, p. 255.

9   'Abdu'l-Bahá, *Selections*, no. 12, p. 27.
10 'Abdu'l-Bahá, *Promulgation*, p. 255.
11 'Abdu'l-Bahá, ibid. p. 58.
12 'Abdu'l-Bahá's complete exposition of the subject is found in *The Promulgation of Universal Peace*, pp. 268–9, and further references on p. 424 of the same book.
13 'Abdu'l-Bahá, *Promulgation*, p. 423.
14 'Abdu'l-Bahá, 'Tablet to Dr. Auguste Henri Forel', in *The Bahá'í World*, vol. 15, p. 40.
15 'Abdu'l-Bahá, *Promulgation*, p. 173.
16 'Abdu'l-Bahá, *Paris Talks*, no. 29, p. 91.
17 ibid. pp. 91–2.
18 'Abdu'l-Bahá, *Some Answered Questions*, no. 59, p. 221.
19 Bahá'u'lláh, *Epistle to the Son of the Wolf*, p. 118.
20 'Abdu'l-Bahá, *Some Answered Questions*, no. 59, p. 220.
21 'Abdu'l-Bahá, *Promulgation*, p. 421.
22 Bahá'u'lláh, *Gleanings*, LXXIII, p. 140.
23 Bahá'u'lláh, *Prayers and Meditations*, no. IV, p. 6.
24 ibid. no. CLXXXI, p. 314 ; and in most Bahá'í prayer books.
25 Bahá'u'lláh, *Gleanings*, XXVI, para. 4, p. 63.
26 'Abdu'l-Bahá, *Promulgation*, p. 422.
27 'Abdu'l-Bahá, 'Tablet to Dr. Auguste Henri Forel', in *The Bahá'í World*, vol. 15, p. 38.
28 Bahá'u'lláh, Lawh-i-Hikmat, in *Tablets*, pp. 140–41.
29 'Abdu'l-Bahá, *Some Answered Questions*, no. 47, p. 181.
30 Bahá'u'lláh, Lawh-i-Hikmat, in *Tablets*, p. 140.
31 Bahá'u'lláh, *Gleanings*, LXXVIII, para. 1, p. 150.
32 Refer also to 'Abdu'l-Bahá, *Foundations of World Unity*, pp. 51–3, 'The Microcosm and the Macrocosm', on the subject of the mystery of creation.
33 'Abdu'l-Bahá, *Some Answered Questions*, no. 47, p. 180.
34 'Abdu'l-Bahá, *Divine Philosophy*, p. 107.
35 'Abdu'l-Bahá, *Promulgation*, p. 219.
36 Bahá'u'lláh, *Gleanings*, CXLVIII, p. 317.
37 'Abdu'l-Bahá, *Promulgation*, p. 274.
38 'Abdu'l-Bahá, *Divine Philosophy*, p. 168.
39 'Abdu'l-Bahá, *Promulgation*, p. 423.
40 Bahá'u'lláh, *Kitáb-i-Íqán*, para. 104, p. 98.
41 Bahá'u'lláh, *Gleanings*, CXLVII, p. 318.
42 'Abdu'l-Bahá, *Promulgation*, p. 422.
43 ibid. p. 165.
44 Bahá'u'lláh, *Gleanings*, XXVII, para. 3, p. 66.
45 Bahá'u'lláh, *Prayers and Meditations*, LXXVII, p. 128.
46 'Abdu'l-Bahá, *Promulgation*, p. 165.
47 John 14: 9–10.
48 Bahá'u'lláh, *Epistle to the Son of the Wolf*, p. 11.
49 Bahá'u'lláh, *Gleanings*, L, p. 103.
50 'Abdu'l-Bahá, *Some Answered Questions*, no. 50, p. 196.
51 'Abdu'l-Bahá, *Foundations of World Unity*, p. 53.

52 Bahá'u'lláh, *Kitáb-i-Íqán*, para. 31, p. 34.
53 'Abdu'l-Bahá, *Promulgation*, p. 257.
54 Bahá'u'lláh, *Hidden Words*, Arabic no. 3.
55 ibid. Arabic no. 11.
56 Bahá'u'lláh, *Gleanings*, XXIX, para. 1, p. 70.
57 Bahá'u'lláh, *Hidden Words*, Arabic no. 5.
58 ibid. Arabic no. 4.
59 ibid. Arabic no. 19.
60 'Abdu'l-Bahá, *Promulgation*, p. 95.
61 Bahá'u'lláh, *Kitáb-i-Íqán*, para. 148, p. 137.
62 Bahá'u'lláh, Kalimát-i-Firdawsíyyih, in *Tablets*, p. 58.
63 'Abdu'l-Bahá, *Promulgation*, pp. 274–5.
64 ibid. p. 422.
65 'Abdu'l-Bahá, *Some Answered Questions*, no. 59, p. 221.
66 Bahá'u'lláh, *Hidden Words*, Arabic no. 67.

3 The soul in this world

1 Bahá'u'lláh, *Gleanings*, LXVII, p. 149.
2 'Abdu'l-Bahá, *Selections*, no. 103, p. 130.
3 'Abdu'l-Bahá, *Promulgation*, p. 465.
4 'Abdu'l-Bahá, *Some Answered Questions*, no. 64, pp. 235–6.
5 'Abdu'l-Bahá, *Selections*, no. 227, p. 302.
6 'Abdu'l-Bahá, *Promulgation*, p. 400.
7 'Abdu'l-Bahá, *Selections*, no. 227, p. 299.
8 'Abdu'l-Bahá, *Promulgation*, pp. 401–2.
9 'Abdu'l-Bahá, *Selections*, no. 68, pp. 103–4.
10 ibid. no. 223, pp. 281–2.
11 ibid. no. 227, p. 302.
12 'Abdu'l-Bahá, *Tablets of the Divine Plan*, p. 24.
13 Bahá'u'lláh, *Epistle to the Son of the Wolf*, pp. 93–4.
14 'Abdu'l-Bahá, *Selections*, no. 143, p. 169.
15 'Abdu'l-Bahá, *Paris Talks*, no. 31, p. 95.
16 ibid. no. 29, p. 89.
17 ibid. p. 93.
18 Shoghi Effendi, letter to an individual believer, 26 October 1932, quoted in *Lights of Guidance*, p. 479.
19 'Abdu'l-Bahá, *Divine Philosophy*, p. 168.
20 Qur'án 29:64 (The Spider).
21 Qur'án 13:26 (Thunder).
22 Bahá'u'lláh, *Gleanings*, LXXX, para. 4, p. 155.
23 'Abdu'l-Bahá, *Some Answered Questions*, no. 66, p. 239.
24 'Abdu'l-Bahá, *Paris Talks*, no. 28, p. 84.
25 'Abdu'l-Bahá, *Promulgation*, p. 60.
26 'Abdu'l-Bahá, *Paris Talks*, no. 29, p. 89.
27 Bahá'u'lláh, *Gleanings*, LXXXII, para. 6, p. 160.
28 ibid. para. 1, pp. 158–9.
29 'Abdu'l-Bahá, *Some Answered Questions*, no. 54, p. 205.

30 ibid. p. 206.
31 ibid. no. 82, p. 294.
32 Shoghi Effendi, letter to an individual believer, 1 April 1946, quoted in *Lights of Guidance*, p. 346.
33 'Abdu'l-Bahá, *Some Answered Questions*, no. 38, p. 151.
34 Letter written on behalf of Shoghi Effendi to an individual, 19 January 1942, quoted in *Lights of Guidance*, p. 209.
35 Bahá'u'lláh, *Gleanings*, LXXXIII, para. 4, pp. 165–6.
36 'Abdu'l-Bahá, *Promulgation*, p. 225.
37 'Abdu'l-Bahá, *Some Answered Questions*, no. 49, p. 194.
38 ibid. no. 51, pp. 198–9.
39 'Abdu'l-Bahá, *Promulgation*, p. 359.
40 'Abdu'l-Bahá, *Selections*, no. 225, pp. 285–6.
41 Shoghi Effendi, *Messages to the Bahá'í World 1950–1957*, p. 74.
42 'Abdu'l-Bahá, *Paris Talks*, no. 23, p. 68.
43 The Báb, *Selections*, p. 157.
44 Bahá'u'lláh, *Hidden Words*, Arabic no. 11.
45 ibid. Arabic no. 12.
46 ibid. Arabic no. 10.
47 'Abdu'l-Bahá, *Promulgation*, p. 4.
48 ibid. p. 49.
49 Bahá'u'lláh, *Hidden Words*, Arabic no. 20.
50 'Abdu'l-Bahá, *Selections*, no. 166, pp. 197–8.
51 Bahá'u'lláh, *Hidden Words*, Arabic no. 15.
52 ibid. Arabic no. 17.

4 Worlds of light

1 'Abdu'l-Bahá, *Tablets*, vol. 2, pp. 249–50.
2 John 14:2.
3 Bahá'u'lláh, Súriy-i-Vafá, in *Tablets*, p. 187.
4 'Abdu'l-Bahá, *Divine Philosophy*, p. 123.
5 'Abdu'l-Bahá, *Memorials of the Faithful*, p. 101.
6 ibid. p. 5.
7 ibid. p. 25.
8 ibid. p. 41.
9 ibid. p. 66.
10 'Abdu'l-Bahá, *Selections*, no. 169, p. 199.
11 ibid. no. 165, p. 197.
12 'Abdu'l-Bahá, *Memorials of the Faithful*, p. 203.
13 ibid. p. 161.
14 ibid. p. 44.
15 ibid. p. 167.
16 'Abdu'l-Bahá, *Tablets*, vol. 2, p. 383.
17 'Abdu'l-Bahá, *Selections*, no. 7, p. 22.
18 'Abdu'l-Bahá, *Tablets*, vol. 1, p. 19.
19 Bahá'u'lláh, *Gleanings*, LXXXI, p. 157.
20 'Abdu'l-Bahá, *'Abdu'l-Bahá in London*, p. 96.

21 'Abdu'l-Bahá, *Promulgation*, p. 90.
22 'Abdu'l-Bahá, *Some Answered Questions*, no. 48, p. 190.
23 'Abdu'l-Bahá, *Tablets*, vol. 1, p. 192.
24 'Abdu'l-Bahá, *Paris Talks*, no. 58, p. 192.
25 'Abdu'l-Bahá, *Tablets*, vol. 2, p. 244.
26 'Abdu'l-Bahá, *Memorials of the Faithful*, p. 17.
27 ibid. p. 22.
28 'Abdu'l-Bahá, *Selections*, no. 146, pp. 174–5.
29 'Abdu'l-Bahá, *Promulgation*, p. 423.
30 Bahá'u'lláh, *Epistle to the Son of the Wolf*, p. 136.
31 Bahá'u'lláh, *Gleanings*, XCIII, paras. 10, 13, p. 189. Emphasis added.
32 ibid. para. 14, p. 190. Emphasis added.
33 Bahá'u'lláh, Lawḥ-i-Ḥikmat, in *Tablets*, p. 142. Emphasis added.
34 Bahá'u'lláh, *Kitáb-i-Íqán*, para. 149, p. 140.
35 Bahá'u'lláh, *Gems of Divine Mysteries*, para. 46, p. 35.
36 Bahá'u'lláh, *Gleanings*, XXVI, para. 1, pp. 60–61.
37 'Abdu'l-Bahá, *Promulgation*, p. 405.
38 Bahá'u'lláh, *Kitáb-i-Íqán*, para. 11, p. 10.
39 ibid. para. 12, p. 11.
40 ibid. para. 17, p. 17–18.
41 'Abdu'l-Bahá, *'Abdu'l-Bahá in London*, p. 62.
42 Bahá'u'lláh, *Gleanings*, XIX, para. 5, p. 48.
43 'Abdu'l-Bahá, *'Abdu'l-Bahá in London*, pp. 66–7.
44 'Abdu'l-Bahá, *Promulgation*, p. 151.
45 'Abdu'l-Bahá, *Some Answered Questions*, no. 14, p. 77.
46 'Abdu'l-Bahá, *Promulgation*, pp. 152–3.
47 Bahá'u'lláh, *Tablets*, p. 268.
48 Bahá'u'lláh, *Gleanings*, XXVII, para. 2, p. 65.
49 ibid. XC, para. 1, p. 177.
50 'Abdu'l-Bahá, *Promulgation*, p. 423.
51 ibid. p. 294.
52 Bahá'u'lláh, *Hidden Words*, Arabic no. 13.
53 'Abdu'l-Bahá, *'Abdu'l-Bahá in London*, p. 80.
54 'Abdu'l-Bahá, *Some Answered Questions*, no. 64, p. 236.
55 ibid. no. 59, p. 222.
56 John 14:9.
57 Qur'án 4:115.
58 John 14:6.
59 'Abdu'l-Bahá, *Promulgation*, p. 94.
60 'Abdu'l-Bahá, *Paris Talks*, no. 27, p. 80.
61 Bahá'u'lláh, *Kitáb-i-Íqán*, para. 52, p. 49.
62 Bahá'u'lláh, *Gleanings*, LXXIV, p. 141.
63 ibid. XLIII, para. 2, p. 92–3.
64 'Abdu'l-Bahá, *Selections*, no. 29, p. 61.
65 Bahá'u'lláh, *Kitáb-i-Aqdas*, para. 148, p. 73.
66 'Abdu'l-Bahá, *Promulgation*, p. 460.

5 Spiritual quickening

1. Bahá'u'lláh, *Gleanings*, CXIII, para. 18, p. 228.
2. 'Abdu'l-Bahá, *Promulgation*, p. 310.
3. ibid. p. 278.
4. ibid. p. 330.
5. Bahá'u'lláh, *Gleanings*, LXXXV, para. 3, p. 169.
6. John 3:6.
7. ibid. 3:3.
8. Qur'án 2:26.
9. ibid. 3:190.
10. Bahá'u'lláh, *Prayers and Meditations*, XXVI, p. 30.
11. 'Abdu'l-Bahá, *Selections*, no. 190, pp. 224–5.
12. Bahá'u'lláh, *Kitáb-i-Íqán*, para. 217, p. 198.
13. Bahá'u'lláh, *Prayers and Meditations*, CXIV, p. 195.
14. John 6:35.
15. 'Abdu'l-Bahá, *Selections*, no. 223, p. 281.
16. Bahá'u'lláh, *Kitáb-i-Aqdas*, para. 39, p. 33.
17. 'Abdu'l-Bahá, *Some Answered Questions*, no. 32, p. 130.
18. 'Abdu'l-Bahá, *Tablets*, vol. 2, p. 269.
19. ibid. p. 308.
20. From a *hadíth* quoted by Bahá'u'lláh, Four Valleys, in *Seven Valleys*, p. 54.
21. Bahá'u'lláh, *Tablets*, pp. 255–6.
22. Bahá'u'lláh, *Gleanings*, CXXVI, para. 3, pp. 271–2.
23. Matt. 22:14.
24. Qur'án 42:12.
25. ibid. 22:55.
26. 'Abdu'l-Bahá, *Selections*, no. 68, p. 104.
27. Bahá'u'lláh, *Prayers and Meditations*, CLXXVI, p. 283.
28. 'Abdu'l-Bahá, *Selections*, no. 236, p. 317.
29. Bahá'u'lláh, *Prayers and Meditations*, CLXXIII, pp. 264–5.
30. Taherzadeh, *The Revelation of Bahá'u'lláh*, vol. 1, p. 118.
31. 'Abdu'l-Bahá, *Foundations of World Unity*, p. 103.
32. Bahá'u'lláh, *Gleanings*, LXX, para. 2, p. 136.
33. 'Abdu'l-Bahá, *Promulgation*, p. 195.
34. 'Abdu'l-Bahá, *'Abdu'l-Bahá in London*, p. 92.
35. 'Abdu'l-Bahá, *Divine Philosophy*, p. 123.
36. 'Abdu'l-Bahá, *Some Answered Questions*, no. 60, pp. 223–4. The Gospel reference is to John 1:13.
37. 'Abdu'l-Bahá, *Paris Talks*, no. 52, p. 176.
38. Bahá'u'lláh, *Kitáb-i-Íqán*, para. 28, p. 29.
39. ibid. para. 29, p. 31.
40. Bahá'u'lláh, Kalimát-i-Firdawsíyyih, in *Tablets*, pp. 63–4.
41. ibid., Ishráqát, p. 125.
42. Shoghi Effendi, 'The Unfoldment of World Civilization', in *The World Order of Bahá'u'lláh*, p. 187.
43. 'Abdu'l-Bahá, *Selections*, no. 7, p. 20.
44. 'Abdu'l-Bahá, *Foundations of World Unity*, p. 103.

45 Bahá'u'lláh, *Gleanings*, LXX, para. 1, p. 136.
46 'Abdu'l-Bahá, *Selections*, no. 16, p. 33.
47 Bahá'u'lláh, Kalimát-i-Firdawsíyyih, in *Tablets*, p. 58.
48 Bahá'u'lláh, *Hidden Words*, Arabic no. 40.
49 ibid. Persian no. 4.
50 Bahá'u'lláh, *Seven Valleys*, p. 39, quoting Jalalu'd-Din Rumi (1207–1273 AD), *The Mathnavi*. Jalalu'd-Din, called Mawlana ('our Master'), is the greatest of all Persian Sufi poets, and founder of the Mawlavi 'whirling' dervish order.
51 'Abdu'l-Bahá, *Selections*, no. 221, p. 277.
52 'Abdu'l-Bahá, *Divine Philosophy*, p. 117.
53 'Abdu'l-Bahá, *Paris Talks*, no. 56, p. 190.
54 'Abdu'l-Bahá, *Promulgation*, pp. 304–5.
55 ibid. p. 279.

6 The effect of veils

1 'Abdu'l-Bahá, *Promulgation*, p. 10.
2 ibid. p. 74.
3 'Abdu'l-Bahá, *Tablets*, vol. 1, p. 19.
4 'Abdu'l-Bahá, *Promulgation*, p. 465.
5 'Abdu'l-Bahá, *Paris Talks*, no. 54, p. 188.
6 'Abdu'l-Bahá, *Promulgation*, p. 90.
7 ibid. p. 91.
8 ibid. p. 60.
9 ibid. p. 14.
10 ibid. p. 244.
11 'Abdu'l-Bahá, *Paris Talks*, no. 34, p. 107.
12 Taherzadeh, *The Revelation of Bahá'u'lláh*, vol. 1, pp. 76–7.
13 Bahá'u'lláh, *Gleanings*, CLIII, para. 8, pp. 328–9.
14 Bahá'u'lláh, *Hidden Words*, Persian no. 41.
15 Bahá'u'lláh, *Kitáb-i-Íqán*, para. 205, p. 188.
16 Bahá'u'lláh, *Tablets*, pp. 235–6.
17 ibid. p. 235.
18 'Abdu'l-Bahá, *Selections*, no. 72, p. 110.
19 Bahá'u'lláh, Aṣl-i-Kullu'l-Khayr (Words of Wisdom), in *Tablets*, p. 156.
20 'Abdu'l-Bahá, *Tablets*, vol. 1, p. 136.
21 ibid. vol. 3, pp. 722–3.
22 Letter on behalf of Shoghi Effendi to an individual believer, 14 December 1941, in *Compilation of Compilations*, vol. 2, p. 11.
23 'Abdu'l-Bahá, *Divine Philosophy*, p. 29.
24 Bahá'u'lláh, *Kitáb-i-Íqán*, para. 53, p. 49.
25 ibid. para. 283, pp. 254–5.
26 Matt. 8:22.
27 'Abdu'l-Bahá, *Promulgation*, p. 459.
28 ibid.
29 Bahá'u'lláh, *Kitáb-i-Íqán*, para. 233, p. 211.
30 'Abdu'l-Bahá, *Promulgation*, pp. 226–7.
31 Bahá'u'lláh, *Gleanings*, XC, para. 1, p. 178, quoting Qu'rán 59:19.

7 Soul, mind and spirit

1. 'Abdu'l-Bahá, *Promulgation*, p. 241.
2. ibid. p. 351.
3. ibid. p. 416.
4. Bahá'u'lláh, *Gleanings*, LXXXIII, para. 4, p. 165.
5. 'Abdu'l-Bahá, *Some Answered Questions*, no. 55, pp. 208–9.
6. See for example 'Abdu'l-Bahá, 'Tablet to Dr. Auguste Henri Forel', in *The Bahá'í World*, vol. 15, pp. 37–43.
7. 'Abdu'l-Bahá, *Paris Talks*, no. 29, p. 92.
8. ibid. p. 88.
9. 'Abdu'l-Bahá, *Tablets*, vol. 3, p. 611.
10. 'Abdu'l-Bahá, *Some Answered Questions*, no. 36, pp. 143–4.
11. ibid. p. 143.
12. ibid. p. 144.
13. 'Abdu'l-Bahá, *Divine Philosophy*, p. 133.
14. See also Chapter 3: 'The soul in this world'.
15. 'Abdu'l-Bahá, *Paris Talks*, no. 31, p. 96.
16. 'Abdu'l-Bahá, *Some Answered Questions*, no. 58, pp. 217–18.
17. 'Abdu'l-Bahá, *Paris Talks*, no. 31, p. 95.
18. ibid. p. 97.
19. 'Abdu'l-Bahá is reported to have said: 'It is the same reality which is given different names, according to the different conditions wherein it becomes manifest. Because of its attachment to matter and the phenomenal world, when it governs the physical functions of the body it is called the human soul. When it manifests itself as the thinker, the comprehender, it is called the mind. And when it soars into the atmosphere of God, and travels in the spiritual world, it becomes designated as spirit' (from the *Diary Notes* of Ahmad Sohrab, February 1914, in *Bahai Scriptures*, pp. 405–6).
20. 'Abdu'l-Bahá, *Some Answered Questions*, no. 56, p. 210.
21. ibid.
22. 'Abdu'l-Bahá, *Tablets*, vol. 2, p. 309.
23. 'Abdu'l-Bahá, *Promulgation*, p. 416.
24. Bahá'u'lláh, *Seven Valleys*, pp. 3–4.
25. 'Abdu'l-Bahá, *Promulgation*, pp. 416–17.
26. Bahá'u'lláh, *Seven Valleys*, p. 32.
27. Bahá'u'lláh, Súriy-i-Vafá, in *Tablets*, pp. 187–8.
28. 'Abdu'l-Bahá, *Promulgation*, pp. 306–7.
29. Bahá'u'lláh, *Seven Valleys*, p. 34, quoting the Imám 'Alí.
30. See 'Abdu'l-Bahá, *Promulgation*, pp. 253–5 and 22–3, where 'Abdu'l-Bahá proves these four methods of acquiring knowledge to be imperfect. See also 'Abdu'l-Bahá, *Some Answered Questions*, no. 55, pp. 207–9.
31. 'Abdu'l-Bahá, *Promulgation*, p. 22.
32. ibid.
33. 'Abdu'l-Bahá, *Some Answered Questions*, no. 55, p. 209.
34. ibid. no. 58, p. 218.
35. 'Abdu'l-Bahá, *Tablets*, vol. 3, p. 549.
36. Bahá'u'lláh, *Gleanings*, XCVIII, para. 1, p. 198.

37 Bahá'u'lláh, *Kitáb-i-Íqán*, para. 2, pp. 3–4.
38 'Abdu'l-Bahá, *Tablets*, vol. 3, p. 506.
39 'Abdu'l-Bahá, *Promulgation*, pp. 338–9.
40 ibid. p. 133.
41 ibid. p. 315.
42 ibid. p. 182.
43 ibid. p. 85.
44 Bahá'u'lláh, *Gleanings*, V, para. 4, p. 8.
45 'Abdu'l-Bahá, *Divine Philosophy*, p. 130.
46 'Abdu'l-Bahá, *Some Answered Questions*, no. 32, p. 130.
47 'Abdu'l-Bahá, *Divine Philosophy*, pp. 131–2.
48 Bahá'u'lláh, *Gleanings*, LXXXII, para. 1, p. 158.
49 'Abdu'l-Bahá, *Divine Philosophy*, p. 130.
50 'Abdu'l-Bahá, *Promulgation*, p. 91.
51 Bahá'u'lláh, Lawḥ-i-Maqṣúd, in *Tablets*, p. 162.
52 'Abdu'l-Bahá, *The Secret of Divine Civilization*, p. 34.
53 'Abdu'l-Bahá, *Promulgation*, p. 59.

8 Mind and the mental faculties

1 'Abdu'l-Bahá, *Divine Philosophy*, p. 95.
2 'Abdu'l-Bahá, *Promulgation*, p. 291.
3 'Abdu'l-Bahá, *Selections*, no. 163, p. 194.
4 'Abdu'l-Bahá, *Promulgation*, p. 360.
5 ibid. p. 351.
6 'Abdu'l-Bahá, *Some Answered Questions*, no. 55, p. 209.
7 'Abdu'l-Bahá, *Divine Philosophy*, p. 121.
8 ibid. p. 102.
9 'Abdu'l-Bahá, *Promulgation*, p. 49.
10 ibid.
11 ibid. p. 351.
12 ibid. p. 49.
13 Bahá'u'lláh, *Gleanings*, XXVI, para. 4, p. 63.
14 From a hadith quoted by Bahá'u'lláh, *Gems of Divine Mysteries*, para. 98, p. 69.
15 Bahá'u'lláh, *Gleanings*, XC, para. 2, p. 178.
16 'Abdu'l-Bahá, *Divine Philosophy*, p. 26.
17 'Abdu'l-Bahá, *Paris Talks*, no. 44, para. 26, p. 150.
18 'Abdu'l-Bahá, *Promulgation*, p. 107.
19 ibid. pp. 360–61.
20 ibid. p. 138.
21 'Abdu'l-Bahá, *Paris Talks*, no. 44, para. 14, p. 147.
22 ibid. para. 23, p. 150.
23 'Abdu'l-Bahá, *Tablets*, vol. 3, p. 506.
24 Bahá'u'lláh, *Gleanings*, CLXIII, para. 2, pp. 342–3.
25 ibid. CX, p. 216.
26 'Abdu'l-Bahá, *Some Answered Questions*, no. 48, p. 186.
27 ibid. no. 74, p. 263.
28 ibid. no. 25, p. 108.

29 ibid. no. 67, p. 242.
30 'Abdu'l-Bahá, *Divine Philosophy*, pp. 127–8.
31 'Abdu'l-Bahá, *Some Answered Questions*, no. 40, p. 157.
32 'Abdu'l-Bahá, 'Tablet to Dr Auguste Henri Forel', p. 38.
33 Bahá'u'lláh, *Gleanings*, LXXX, para. 2, pp. 153–4.
34 'Abdu'l-Bahá, 'Tablet to Dr Auguste Henri Forel', p. 43.
35 Bahá'u'lláh, *The Kitáb-i-Aqdas*, para. 155, p. 75.
36 'Abdu'l-Bahá, Tablets quoted ibid., note 170, pp. 238–9.
37 'Abdu'l-Bahá, *Selections*, no. 21, pp. 48–9.
38 'Abdu'l-Bahá's Tablet to Dr Auguste Forel is the most comprehensive single commentary on the soul and mind in the Writings, and a number of excerpts from that Tablet are included in this compilation.
39 'Abdu'l-Bahá, 'Tablet to Dr Auguste Henri Forel', p. 42.
40 'Abdu'l-Bahá, *Some Answered Questions*, no. 58, pp. 217–18.
41 'Abdu'l-Bahá, *Selections*, no. 126, pp. 144–5.
42 'Abdu'l-Bahá, *Promulgation*, p. 310.
43 ibid. p. 108.
44 ibid. p. 49.
45 ibid. p. 297.
46 Letter written on behalf of Shoghi Effendi, 7 June 1946, in *Arohanui*, no. 75, p. 85.
47 'Abdu'l-Bahá, *The Secret of Divine Civilization*, p. 1.

9 The struggle within

1 'Abdu'l-Bahá, *Promulgation*, p. 287.
2 'Abdu'l-Bahá, in *Bahá'í Readings*, p. 305; from provisional translation in *Bahai Scriptures* (1923), no. 986, p. 546.
3 Bahá'u'lláh, in *Bahá'í Prayers*, p. 144.
4 ibid. p. 121.
5 Bahá'u'lláh, *Gleanings*, CLIII, para. 6, p. 327.
6 'Abdu'l-Bahá, *Tablets*, vol. 1, p. 109.
7 Bahá'u'lláh, *Gleanings*, CV, para. 6, p. 212.
8 ibid., CII, p. 206.
9 Bahá'u'lláh, *Hidden Words*, Persian no. 27.
10 ibid. Arabic no. 59.
11 ibid. Persian no. 31.
12 'Abdu'l-Bahá, *Promulgation*, p. 15.
13 Bahá'u'lláh, *Tablets*, p. 172.
14 Letter written on behalf of Shoghi Effendi to an individual, 26 December 1935, in *Lights of Guidance*, p. 550.
15 'Abdu'l-Bahá, *Promulgation*, p. 296.
16 ibid. p. 309.
17 ibid. p. 465.
18 'Abdu'l-Bahá, *Some Answered Questions*, no. 29, p. 118.
19 'Abdu'l-Bahá, *Promulgation*, pp. 465–6.
20 'Abdu'l-Bahá, *Some Answered Questions*, no. 64, p. 237.
21 ibid. no. 62, p. 230.

22 ibid. no. 52, p. 200.
23 ibid. no. 70, p. 248.
24 Bahá'u'lláh, *Gleanings*, CLIX, para. 2, p. 336.
25 'Abdu'l-Bahá, *Paris Talks*, no. 18, p. 55.
26 'Abdu'l-Bahá, *Divine Philosophy*, pp. 120–21.
27 Bahá'u'lláh, *Gleanings*, CXXVIII, para. 4, p. 276.
28 I Tim. 6:10.
29 Taherzadeh, *The Covenant of Bahá'u'lláh*, p. 8.
30 'Abdu'l-Bahá, *'Abdu'l-Bahá in London*, p. 87.
31 Bahá'u'lláh, *Gleanings*, CLIII, para. 8, p. 328.
32 'Abdu'l-Bahá, *Selections*, no. 150, p. 178.
33 Bahá'u'lláh, *Gleanings*, CXVIII, para. 7, p. 252.
34 'Abdu'l-Bahá, *Selections*, no. 1, p. 3.
35 'Abdu'l-Bahá, *Tablets of the Divine Plan*, p. 15.
36 Bahá'u'lláh, *Gleanings*, CIII, para. 4, p. 209.
37 Bahá'u'lláh, Súriy-i-Haykal, para. 260, in *Summons of the Lord of Hosts*, p. 130.
38 Bahá'u'lláh, *Gleanings*, LXXI, para. 3, p. 138.
39 ibid. CXXIII, para. 2, p. 261.
40 I Tim. 6:7.
41 Bahá'u'lláh, *Gleanings*, LXVI, para. 4, p. 127.

10 To seek and to find

1   'Abdu'l-Bahá, *Paris Talks*, no. 38, p. 120.
2   Bahá'u'lláh, *Gleanings*, LXXV, para. 1, p. 43.
3   'Abdu'l-Bahá, *Paris Talks*, no. 41, pp. 139–141.
4   Bahá'u'lláh, *Kitáb-i-Íqán*, para. 213, p. 192.
5   Jer. 29:13.
6   Luke 11:9–10.
7   'Abdu'l-Bahá, *Tablets,* vol. 1, p. 204.
8   Bahá'u'lláh, *Tablets*, p. 255.
9   Bahá'u'lláh, *Gems of Divine Mysteries*, para. 55, pp. 40–41.
10 Bahá'u'lláh, *Prayers and Meditations*, CLVI, p. 250.
11 ibid. LVI, p. 82.
12 Bahá'u'lláh, Súriy-i-Haykal, in *Summons of the Lord of Hosts*, pp. 103–4.
13 Bahá'u'lláh, *Hidden Words*, Persian no. 38.
14 Isa. 40:31.
15 Bahá'u'lláh, *Kitáb-i-Íqán*, para. 216, pp. 195–6.
16 'Abdu'l-Bahá, *Tablets*, vol. 2, p. 396.
17 Bahá'u'lláh, *Gleanings*, CLIII, para. 5, p. 326.
18 Bahá'u'lláh, *Kitáb-i-Íqán*, para. 44, p. 43.
19 Bahá'u'lláh, *The Seven Valleys and The Four Valleys*, p. 15.
20 Bahá'u'lláh, *Kitáb-i-Íqán*, para. 167, pp. 157–8. The word 'Riḍván' (Persian) may be translated as 'heaven'.
21 'Abdu'l-Bahá, *Paris Talks*, no. 17, p. 52.
22 'Abdu'l-Bahá, *Tablets*, vol. 3, pp. 706–7.
23 Bahá'u'lláh, *Kitáb-i-Íqán*, para. 163–4, pp. 156–7.
24 Bahá'u'lláh, Four Valleys, in *The Seven Valleys and The Four Valleys*, p. 58.

25 Bahá'u'lláh, *Epistle to the Son of the Wolf*, p. 32.
26 'Abdu'l-Bahá, *Promulgation*, p. 53.
27 Bahá'u'lláh, Lawḥ-i-Dunyá, in *Tablets*, p. 93.
28 Bahá'u'lláh, *Gleanings*, CXXVI, para. 4, p. 272.
29 Bahá'u'lláh, Kalimát-i-Firdawsíyyih, in *Tablets*, p. 63.

11 The source of happiness

1 'Abdu'l-Bahá, *Selections*, no. 100, p. 127.
2 ibid. no. 103, pp. 130–31.
3 'Abdu'l-Bahá, *Promulgation*, p. 157.
4 'Abdu'l-Bahá, *Paris Talks*, no. 2, p. 4.
5 ibid. no. 26, p. 78.
6 'Abdu'l-Bahá, *Tablets*, vol. 3, p. 638.
7 ibid. pp. 695–6.
8 'Abdu'l-Bahá, *Divine Philosophy*, p. 122.
9 'Abdu'l-Bahá, *Tablets*, vol. 2, p. 324.
10 'Abdu'l-Bahá, *Selections*, no. 155, pp. 181–2.
11 Bahá'u'lláh, *Gleanings*, XXIX, para. 3, p. 71.
12 ibid. para. 2, p. 71.
13 Bahá'u'lláh, *Kitáb-i-Íqán*, para. 8, pp. 8–9.
14 'Abdu'l-Bahá, *Paris Talks*, no. 57, p. 191.
15 ibid. no. 14, p. 43.
16 ibid. p. 42.
17 Letter written on behalf of Shoghi Effendi to an individual, 29 May 1935, in *Unfolding Destiny*, p. 434.
18 'Abdu'l-Bahá, *Promulgation of Universal Peace*, pp. 451–2.
19 Bahá'u'lláh, *Seven Valleys*, pp. 13–15.
20 'Abdu'l-Bahá, *Paris Talks*, no. 35, pp. 110–12.
21 'Abdu'l-Bahá, *Divine Art of Living*, p. 18.
22 'Abdu'l-Bahá, *Tablets*, vol. 2, p. 263.
23 ibid. vol. 1, p. 98.
24 'Abdu'l-Bahá, *Promulgation*, p. 335.
25 Letter written on behalf of Shoghi Effendi to an individual, 23 December 1948, in *Unfolding Destiny*, p. 453.
26 Bahá'u'lláh, *Gleanings*, XXVI, para. 2, p. 61.
27 'Abdu'l-Bahá, *Promulgation*, p. 38.
28 ibid. p. 349.
29 The Báb, Persian Bayán IV:12, in *Selections*, p. 106.
30 Bahá'u'lláh, *Gleanings*, XXXVIII, pp. 87–8.
31 'Abdu'l-Bahá, *Paris Talks*, no. 2, p. 4.
32 Prov. 23:7.
33 'Abdu'l-Bahá, *Divine Philosophy*, p. 171.
34 Letter written on behalf of Shoghi Effendi to an individual, 19 October 1947, in *Unfolding Destiny*, p. 448.
35 'Abdu'l-Bahá, *Selections*, no. 188, pp. 217–18.
36 'Abdu'l-Bahá, *Paris Talks*, no. 35, p. 111.
37 'Abdu'l-Bahá, *Tablets*, vol. 1, p. 67.

38 Bahá'u'lláh, *Prayers and Meditations*, CIX, p. 183.
39 'Abdu'l-Bahá, *A Traveler's Narrative*, p. 73.
40 Bahá'u'lláh, Súriy-i-Vafá, in *Tablets*, p. 190.
41 Bahá'u'lláh, *Epistle to the Son of the Wolf*, pp. 8–9.
42 Bahá'u'lláh, *Gleanings*, CXIV, para. 4, p. 233.
43 Bahá'u'lláh, *Prayers and Meditations*, CLXII, p. 255.
44 Bahá'u'lláh, in *Bahá'í World*, vol. 18, p. 10.
45 'Abdu'l-Bahá, *Paris Talks*, no. 34, pp. 108–9.
46 'Abdu'l-Bahá, *Promulgation*, p. 131.
47 'Abdu'l-Bahá, *Selections*, no. 150, p. 178.
48 The Báb, *Selections*, p. 193.

12 Departing this life

1 Bahá'u'lláh, *Gleanings*, LXXXI, p. 157.
2 'Abdu'l-Bahá, *Promulgation*, p. 226.
3 Taherzadeh, *The Covenant of Bahá'u'lláh*, p. 11.
4 'Abdu'l-Bahá, *Selections*, no. 145, pp. 169–70.
5 ibid. no. 163, p. 193.
6 ibid. p. 195.
7 'Abdu'l-Bahá, *'Abdu'l-Bahá in London*, p. 96.
8 'Abdu'l-Bahá, *Promulgation*, p. 270.
9 'Abdu'l-Bahá, *Star of the West*, vol. 19, no. 3, p. 69, quoted in 'The Importance of Deepening Our Knowledge and Understanding of the Faith', in *Compilation of Compilations*, vol. 1, no. 425, p. 202.
10 'Abdu'l-Bahá, *Paris Talks*, no. 31, p. 98.
11 ibid. no. 54, p. 188.
12 'Abdu'l-Bahá, *Some Answered Questions*, no. 61, p. 228.
13 'Abdu'l-Bahá, *Selections*, no. 149, p. 177.
14 ibid. no. 145, p. 170.
15 The Báb, Persian Bayán V:12, in *Selections*, p. 95.
16 Bahá'u'lláh, *Gleanings*, LXXXI, p. 157.
17 'Abdu'l-Bahá, *Some Answered Questions*, no. 67, p. 241.
18 Bahá'u'lláh, *Gleanings*, LXXXVI, para. 4, p. 171.
19 'Abdu'l-Bahá, *Selections*, no. 156, p. 185.
20 'Abdu'l-Bahá, *Promulgation*, pp. 47–8.
21 'Abdu'l-Bahá, *Selections*, no. 171, p. 201.
22 ibid. no. 169, pp. 199–200.
23 'Abdu'l-Bahá, in *Bahá'í Prayers*, pp. 45–6.
24 Bahá'u'lláh, *Gleanings*, LXXV, p. 143.
25 'Abdu'l-Bahá, *Some Answered Questions*, no. 66, p. 240.
26 ibid. no. 62, p. 231.
27 ibid.
28 ibid. p. 232.
29 'Abdu'l-Bahá, *Selections*, no. 149, p. 177.
30 Bahá'u'lláh, *Gleanings*, LXXX, para. 3, p. 154.
31 'Abdu'l-Bahá, *Tablets*, vol. 1, p. 205.
32 ibid. p. 206.

33 'Abdu'l-Bahá, *Selections*, no. 163, p. 194.
34 'Abdu'l-Bahá, *Promulgation*, pp. 464–5.
35 Bahá'u'lláh, *Gleanings*, LXXXI, p. 157.

13 Life notes for the pilgrim

1 'Abdu'l-Bahá, *Selections*, no. 176, pp. 204–5.
2 'Abdu'l-Bahá, *'Abdu'l-Bahá in London*, p. 120.
3 'Abdu'l-Bahá, *Paris Talks*, no. 26, p. 78.
4 ibid. no. 54, pp. 187–8.
5 'Abdu'l-Bahá, *Selections*, no. 40, p. 82.
6 Bahá'u'lláh, *Epistle to the Son of the Wolf*, p. 137.
7 ibid. p. 17.
8 'Abdu'l-Bahá, *Tablets*, vol. 2, p. 297.
9 ibid. pp. 312–13.
10 ibid. pp. 265–6.
11 'Abdu'l-Bahá, *'Abdu'l-Bahá in London*, p. 121.
12 'Abdu'l-Bahá, *Selections*, no. 150, p. 178.
13 Reported words of 'Abdu'l-Bahá in the course of His parting address to the first group of western pilgrims who visited Him in 'Akká in 1898–99, in Maxwell, *An Early Pilgrimage*, p. 40.
14 Bahá'u'lláh, Lawḥ-i-Maqṣúd, in *Tablets*, p. 176.
15 'Abdu'l-Bahá, *Selections*, no. 22, p. 51.

14 Bahá'u'lláh and the evolution of spiritual man

1 Micah 7:12.
2 Shoghi Effendi, *God Passes By*, p. 94.
3 Bahá'u'lláh, *Kitáb-i-Íqán*, para. 106, pp. 99–100.
4 ibid. para. 110, pp. 103–4.
5 Bahá'u'lláh, *Gleanings*, CVI, para. 1, p. 213.
6 Bahá'u'lláh, Lawḥ-i-Maqṣúd, in *Tablets*, p. 167.
7 'Abdu'l-Bahá, *Promulgation*, p. 220.
8 Shoghi Effendi, *The Promised Day Is Come*, p. 4.
9 ibid. p. 112.
10 Shoghi Effendi, *Messages to the Bahá'í World*, p. 103.
11 Bahá'u'lláh, *Kitáb-i-Íqán*, para. 270, pp. 240–41.
12 Bahá'u'lláh, *Gleanings*, CX, p. 216.
13 Bahá'u'lláh, *Epistle to the Son of the Wolf*, p. 62.
14 Bahá'u'lláh, *Gleanings*, XVI, para. 3, pp. 39–40.
15 ibid. XXXIV, para. 6, p. 80.
16 ibid. CVI, para. 1, p. 213.
17 ibid. XXXIV, para. 6, p. 80.
18 ibid. CXXXI, para. 2, p. 286.
19 ibid. LXX, para. 2, p. 136.
20 'Abdu'l-Bahá, *Promulgation*, p. 396.
21 Bahá'u'lláh, quoted by Shoghi Effendi, 'The Unfoldment of World Civilization', in *The World Order of Bahá'u'lláh*, p. 186.
22 Bahá'u'lláh, *Gleanings*, CXX, para. 3, p. 255.

23 ibid. XXXIV, para. 6, p. 81.
24 Shoghi Effendi, 'The Unfoldment of World Civilization', in *The World Order of Bahá'u'lláh*, p. 163.
25 Shoghi Effendi, 'The Goal of a New World Order', in *The World Order of Bahá'u'lláh*, pp. 42–3.
26 Bahá'u'lláh, I<u>sh</u>ráqát, in *Tablets*, p. 125.
27 Shoghi Effendi, *Citadel of Faith*, p. 125.
28 Shoghi Effendi, 'The Unfoldment of World Civilization', in *The World Order of Bahá'u'lláh*, p. 187.
29 ibid. p. 186.
30 Shoghi Effendi, 'The Goal of a New World Order', in *The World Order of Bahá'u'lláh*, p. 43.
31 Bahá'u'lláh, *Gleanings*, CXXXII, para. 3, p. 288.
32 Taherzadeh, *The Revelation of Bahá'u'lláh*, vol. 2, p. 251.
33 Shoghi Effendi, *The Promised Day Is Come*, pp. 117–18.
34 'Abdu'l-Bahá, *Promulgation*, p. 220.
35 'Abdu'l-Bahá, *Some Answered Questions*, no. 41, p. 160.
36 Bahá'u'lláh, *Gleanings*, LXXXVII, para. 1, p. 172.
37 'Abdu'l-Bahá, *Promulgation*, p. 295.
38 'Abdu'l-Bahá, *Some Answered Questions*, no. 51, pp. 198–9. See also Chapter 3 of this book: 'The soul in this world'.
39 ibid. p. 199.
40 Bahá'u'lláh, *The Kitáb-i-Aqdas*, para. 5, p. 21.
41 Bahá'u'lláh, Tajallíyát, in *Tablets*, p. 50.